Praise for
In Defense of a Liberal Education

"[Zakaria's] argument could not come at a more important time."
                                                  —*New Republic*

"Surprising and welcome. . . . A compact, effective essay on the importance of a broad, contextual education. Cheerfully out of step with the strident critics of higher ed, *In Defense of a Liberal Education* is a reminder that American colleges and universities are a powerful resource that has allowed so many young people to learn about themselves and their ability to have a positive impact on the world."
                                                  —*Daily Beast*

"Zakaria is spot on in his dismay toward contemporary pressures for technical-mastery, skills-based learning that is narrow, linear, and jobist. Not that jobs are a bad thing at all. Zakaria would simply say that this is probably not the best path, and there is a considerable data to back him up."
                                                  —*New York Journal of Books*

In Defense of a
Liberal Education

Also by Fareed Zakaria

The Post-American World

*The Future of Freedom: Illiberal Democracy
at Home and Abroad*

*From Wealth to Power: The Unusual Origins
of America's World Role*

*The American Encounter: The United States and the
Making of the Modern World* (coeditor)

In Defense of a Liberal Education

FAREED ZAKARIA

W. W. NORTON & COMPANY

Independent Publishers Since 1923

New York • London

For information about permission to reproduce selections from
this book, write to Permissions, W. W. Norton & Company, Inc.,
500 Fifth Avenue, New York, NY 10110

For information about special discounts for bulk purchases,
please contact W. W. Norton Special Sales at
specialsales@wwnorton.com or 800-233-4830

Manufacturing by RR Donnelley
Production manager: Julia Druskin

Library of Congress Cataloging-in-Publication Data

Zakaria, Fareed.
In defense of a liberal education / Fareed Zakaria.
pages cm
Includes bibliographical references.
ISBN 978-0-393-24768-8 (hardcover)
1. Education, Humanistic. I. Title.
LC1011.Z34 2015
370.11'2—dc23

2014043268

ISBN 978-0-393-35234-4 pbk.

W. W. Norton & Company, Inc.
500 Fifth Avenue, New York, N.Y. 10110
www.wwnorton.com

W. W. Norton & Company Ltd.
Castle House, 75/76 Wells Street, London W1T 3QT

1 2 3 4 5 6 7 8 9 0

For my children,
Omar, Lila, and Sofia

We are drowning in information, while starving for wisdom. The world henceforth will be run by synthesizers, people able to put together the right information at the right time, think critically about it, and make important choices wisely.

—E. O. Wilson

Contents

1: Coming to America   15

2: A Brief History of Liberal Education   40

3: Learning to Think   72

4: The Natural Aristocracy   106

5: Knowledge and Power   135

6: In Defense of Today's Youth   150

Notes   171

Acknowledgments   201

In Defense of a
Liberal Education

1

Coming to America

IF YOU WANT to live a good life these days, you know what you're supposed to do. Get into college but then drop out. Spend your days learning computer science and your nights coding. Start a technology company and take it public. That's the new American dream. If you're not quite that adventurous, you could major in electrical engineering.

What you are not supposed to do is study the liberal arts. Around the world, the idea of a broad-based "liberal" education is closely tied to the United States and its great universities and colleges. But in America itself, a liberal education is out of favor.

In an age defined by technology and globalization, everyone is talking about skills-based learning. Politicians, businesspeople, and even many educators see it as the only way for the nation to stay competitive. They urge students to stop dreaming and start thinking practically about the skills they will need in the workplace. An open-ended exploration of knowledge is seen as a road to nowhere.

A classic liberal education has few defenders. Conservatives fume that it is too, well, liberal (though the term has no partisan meaning). Liberals worry it is too elitist. Students wonder what they would do with a degree in psychology. And parents fear that it will cost them their life savings.

This growing unease is apparent in the numbers. As college enrollment has grown in recent decades, the percentage of students majoring in subjects like English and philosophy has declined sharply. In 1971, for example, 7.6 percent of all bachelor's degrees were awarded in English language and literature. By 2012, that number had fallen to 3.0 percent. During the same period, the percentage of business majors in the undergraduate population rose from 13.7 to 20.5.

Some believe this pattern makes sense—that new entrants into higher education might simply prefer job training to the liberal arts. Perhaps. But in earlier periods of educational expansion, this was not the case. In the 1950s and 1960s, for instance, students saw college as more than a glorified trade school. Newcomers, often from lower-middle-class backgrounds and immigrant families with little education, enthusiastically embraced the liberal arts. They saw it as a gateway to a career, and also as a way to assimilate into American culture. "I have to speak absolutely perfect English," says Philip Roth's character Alex Portnoy, the son of immigrants and hero of the novel *Portnoy's Complaint*. Majors like English and history grew in popularity precisely during the decades of mass growth in American higher education.

The great danger facing American higher education is *not* that too many students are studying the liberal arts. Here are the data. In the 2011–12 academic year, 52 percent of American undergraduates were enrolled in two-year or less-than-two-year colleges, and 48 percent were enrolled in four-year institutions. At two-year colleges, the most popular area of study was health professions and related sciences (23.3 percent). An additional 11.7 percent of students studied business, management, and marketing. At four-year colleges, the pattern was the same. Business led the list of majors, accounting for 18.9 percent of students, and health was second, accounting for 13.4 percent.

Another estimate found that only a third of all bachelor's degree recipients study fields that could be classified as the liberal arts. And only about 1.8 percent of all undergraduates attend classic liberal arts colleges like Amherst, Swarthmore, and Pomona.

As you can see, we do not have an oversupply of students studying history, literature, philosophy, or physics and math for that matter. A majority is specializing in fields because they see them as directly related to the job market. It's true that more Americans need technical training, and all Americans need greater scientific literacy. But the drumbeat of talk about skills and jobs has not lured people into engineering and biology—not everyone has the aptitude for science—so much as it has made them nervously forsake the humanities and take courses in business and communications. Many of these students might well have been better off taking a richer, deeper set of courses in subjects they found fascinating—and supplementing it, as we all should, with some basic knowledge of computers and math. In any event, what is clear is that the gap in technical training is not being caused by the small percentage of students who choose four-year degrees in the liberal arts.

Whatever the facts, the assaults continue and have moved from the realm of rhetoric to action. The governors of Texas, Florida, North Carolina, and Wisconsin have announced that they do not intend to keep subsidizing the liberal arts at state-funded universities. "Is it a vital interest of the state to have more anthropologists?" Florida's Rick Scott asked. "I don't think so." Wisconsin is planning to cut money from subjects that don't train students for a specific job right out of college. "How many PhDs in philosophy do I need to subsidize?" the radio show host William Bennett asked North Carolina's Patrick McCrory, a sentiment with which McCrory enthusiastically agreed. (Ironically, Bennett himself has a PhD in philosophy, which appears to have trained him well for his multiple careers in government, media, nonprofits, and the private sector.)

It isn't only Republicans on the offensive. Everyone's eager to promote the type of education that might lead directly to a job. In a speech in January 2014, President Barack Obama said, "I promise you, folks can make a lot more, potentially, with skilled manufacturing or the trades than they might with an art history degree." He later apologized for what he described as a "glib" comment, but Obama has expressed similar sentiments during his presidency. His concern—that in today's world, college graduates need to focus on the tools that will get them good jobs—is shared by many liberals, as well as conservatives and independents. The irrelevance of a liberal education is an idea that has achieved that rare status in Washington: bipartisan agreement.

The attacks have an effect. There is today a loss of coherence and purpose surrounding the idea of a liberal education. Its proponents are defensive about its virtues, while its opponents are convinced that it is at best an expensive luxury, at worst actively counterproductive. Does it really make sense to study English in the age of apps?

In a sense, the question is un-American. For much of its history, America was distinctive in providing an education to all that was *not* skills based. In their comprehensive study of education, the Harvard economists Claudia Goldin and Lawrence Katz note that, historically, Britain, France, and Germany tested children at a young age, educated only a few, and put them through a narrow program designed specifically to impart a set of skills thought to be key to their professions. "The American system," they write, "can be characterized as open, forgiving, lacking universal standards, and having an academic yet practical curriculum." America did not embrace the European model of specific training and apprenticeships because Americans moved constantly, to new cities,

counties, and territories in search of new opportunities. They were not rooted in geographic locations with
long-established trades and guilds that offered the only
path forward. They were also part of an economy that
was new and dynamic, so that technology kept changing the nature of work and with it the requirements
for jobs. Few wanted to lock themselves into a single
industry for life. Finally, Goldin and Katz argue, while
a general education was more expensive than specialized training, the cost for the former was not paid by
students or their parents. The United States was the
first country to publicly fund mass, general education,
first at the secondary-school level and then in college.
Even now, higher education in America is a much
broader and richer universe than anywhere else. Today
a high school student can go to one of fourteen hundred institutions in the United States that offer a traditional bachelor's degree, and another fifteen hundred
with a more limited course of study. Goldin and Katz
point out that on a per capita basis, Britain has only
half as many undergraduate institutions and Germany
just one-third. Those who seek to reorient U.S. higher
education into something more focused and technical
should keep in mind that they would be abandoning
what has been historically distinctive, even unique, in
the American approach to higher education.

And yet, I get it. I understand America's current obsession. I grew up in India in the 1960s and 1970s, when a skills-based education was seen as the only path to a good career. Indians in those days had an almost mystical faith in the power of technology. It had been embedded in the country's DNA since it gained independence in 1947. Jawaharlal Nehru, India's first prime minister, was fervent in his faith in big engineering projects. He believed that India could move out of its economic backwardness only by embracing technology, and he did everything he could during his fourteen years in office to leave that stamp on the nation. A Fabian socialist, Nehru had watched with admiration as the Soviet Union jump-started its economy in just a few decades by following such a path. (Lenin once famously remarked, "Communism is Soviet power plus the electrification of the whole country.") Nehru described India's new hydro-electric dams as "temples of the new age."

I attended a private day school in Bombay (now Mumbai), the Cathedral and John Connon School. When founded by British missionaries in the Victorian era, the school had been imbued with a broad, humanistic approach to education. It still had some of that outlook when I was there, but the country's mood was feverishly practical. The 1970s was a tough decade everywhere economically, but especially in India. And though it was a private school, the tuition was low, and Cathedral catered to a broad cross section of the middle class. As a result, all my peers and their parents were anxious about job prospects. The assumption made by almost everyone at school was that engineering and medicine were the two best careers. The real question was, which one would you pursue?

At age sixteen, we had to choose one of three academic streams: science, commerce, or the humanities. We all took a set of board exams that year—a remnant of the British educational model—that helped determine our trajectory. In those days, the choices were obvious. The smart kids would go into science, the rich kids would do commerce, and the girls would take the humanities. (Obviously I'm exaggerating, but not by that much.) Without giving the topic much thought, I streamed into the sciences.

At the end of twelfth grade, we took another set of exams. These were the big ones. They determined our educational future, as we were reminded again and again. Grades in school, class participation, extracurricular projects, and teachers' recommendations—all were deemed irrelevant compared to the exam scores. Almost all colleges admitted students based solely on these numbers. In fact, engineering colleges asked for scores in only three subjects: physics, chemistry, and mathematics. Similarly, medical schools would ask for results in just physics, chemistry, and biology. No one cared what you got in English literature. The Indian Institutes of Technology (IITs)—the most prestigious engineering colleges in the country—narrowed the admissions criteria even further. They administered their own entrance test, choosing applicants entirely on the basis of its results.

The increased emphasis on technology and practicality in the 1970s was in part due to domestic factors: inflation had soared, the economy had slumped, and the private sector was crippled by nationalizations and regulations. Another big shift, however, took place far from India's borders. Until the 1970s, the top British universities offered scholarships to bright Indian students—a legacy of the raj. But as Britain went through its own hellish economic times that decade—placed under formal receivership in 1979 by the International Monetary Fund—money for foreign scholarships dried up. In an earlier era, some of the brightest graduates from India might have gone on to Oxford, Cambridge, and the University of London. Without outside money to pay for that education, they stayed home.

But culture follows power. As Britain's economic decline made its universities less attractive, colleges in the United States were rising in wealth and ambition. At my school, people started to notice that American universities had begun offering generous scholarships to foreign students. And we soon began to hear from early trailblazers about the distinctly American approach to learning. A friend from my neighborhood who had gone to Cornell came back in the summers bursting with enthusiasm about his time there. He told us of the incredible variety of courses that students could take no matter what their major. He also told tales of the richness of college life. I remember listening to him describe a film society at Cornell that held screenings and discussions of classics by Ingmar Bergman and Federico Fellini. I had never heard of Bergman or Fellini, but I was amazed that watching movies was considered an integral part of higher education. Could college really be that much fun?

My parents did not push me to specialize. My father had been deeply interested in history and politics ever since he was a young boy. He had been orphaned at a young age but managed to get financial assistance that put him through high school and college. In 1944, he received a scholarship to attend the University of London. He arrived during the worst of the blitzkrieg, with German V-2 rockets raining down on the city. On the long boat ride to England, the crew told him he was crazy. One member even asked, "Haven't you read the newspapers? People are leaving London by the thousands right now. Why would you go there?" But my father was determined to get an education. History was his passion, and he worked toward a PhD in that subject. But he needed a clearer path to a profession. So, in addition, he obtained a law degree that would allow him to become a barrister upon his return to Bombay.

Though my mother was raised in better circumstances, she also faced a setback at a young age—her father died when she was eight. She briefly attended a college unusual for India at the time—a liberal arts school in the northern part of the country called the Isabella Thoburn College, founded in 1870 by an American Methodist missionary of that name. Though her education was cut short when she returned home to look after her widowed mother, my mother never forgot the place. She often fondly reminisced about its broad and engaging curriculum.

My parents' careers were varied and diverse. My father started out as a lawyer before moving into politics and later founding a variety of colleges. He also created a small manufacturing company (to pay the bills) and always wrote books and essays. My mother began as a social worker and then became a journalist, working for newspapers and magazines. (She resigned from her last position in journalism last year, 2014, at the age of seventy-eight.) Neither of them insisted on early specialization. In retrospect, my parents must have worried about our future prospects—everyone else was worried. But to our good fortune, they did not project that particular anxiety on us.

My brother, Arshad, took the first big step. He was two years older than I and fantastically accomplished academically. (He was also a very good athlete, which made following in his footsteps challenging.) He had the kind of scores on his board exams that would have easily placed him in the top engineering programs in the country. Or he could have taken the IIT exam, which he certainly would have aced. In fact, he decided not to do any of that and instead applied to American universities. A couple of his friends considered doing the same, but no one quite knew how the process worked. We learned, for example, that applicants had to take something called the Scholastic Aptitude Test, but we didn't know much about it. (Remember, this is 1980 in India. There was no Google. In fact, there was no color television.) We found a pamphlet about the test at the United States Information Service, the cultural branch of the U.S. embassy. It said that because the SAT was an aptitude test, there was no need to study for it. So, my brother didn't. On the day the test was scheduled, he walked into the makeshift exam center in Bombay, an almost empty room in one of the local colleges, and took the test.

It's difficult to convince people today how novel and risky an idea it was at the time to apply to schools in the United States. The system was still foreign and distant. People didn't really know what it meant to get into a good American university or how that would translate into a career in India. The Harvard alumni in Bombay in the 1970s were by no means a "Who's Who" of the influential and wealthy. Rather, they were an eclectic mix of people who either had spent time abroad (because their parents had foreign postings) or had some connection to America. A few friends of ours had ventured to the United States already, but because they hadn't yet graduated or looked for jobs, their experiences were of little guidance.

My brother had no idea if the admissions departments at American colleges would understand the Indian system or know how to interpret his report cards and recommendations. He also had no real Plan B. If he didn't take the slot offered by engineering schools, he wouldn't be able to get back in line the next year. In fact, things were so unclear to us that we didn't even realize American colleges required applications a full year in advance. As a result, he involuntarily took a gap year between school and college, waiting around to find out whether he got in anywhere.

As it happened, Arshad got in everywhere. He picked the top of the heap—accepting a scholarship offer from Harvard. While we were all thrilled and impressed, many friends remained apprehensive when told the news. It sounded prestigious to say you were going to attend Harvard, but would the education actually translate into a career?

My mother traveled to the United States to drop my brother off in the fall of 1981, an uneasy time in American history. The mood was still more 1970s malaise than 1980s boom. The country was in the midst of the worst recession since the Great Depression. Vietnam and Watergate had shattered the nation's confidence. The Soviet Union was seen as ascendant in our minds. Riots, protests, and urban violence had turned American cities into places of genuine danger. Our images of New York came from Charles Bronson movies and news reports of crack and crime.

All of this was especially alarming to Indians. The country's traditional society had interpreted the 1960s and 1970s as a period of decay in American culture, as young people became morally lax, self-indulgent, permissive, and, perhaps most worrisome, rebellious. The idea that American youth had become disrespectful toward their elders was utterly unnerving to Indian parents. Most believed that any child who traveled to the United States would quickly cast aside family, faith, and tradition for sex, drugs, and rock and roll. If you sent your kids to America, you had to brace yourselves for the prospect that you might "lose" them.

In his first few weeks abroad, Arshad was, probably like all newcomers to Harvard, a bit nervous. My mother, on the other hand, returned from her trip clear of any anxiety. She was enchanted with the United States, its college campuses, and the undergraduate experience. She turned her observations into an article for the *Times of India* titled "The Other America." In it, she described how concerned she had been before the trip about permissiveness, drugs, and rebellion at American colleges. She then went on to explain how impressed she was after actually spending time on a campus to find that the place focused on education, hard work, and extracurricular activities. The students she met were bright, motivated, and, to her surprise, quite respectful. She met parents who were tearfully bidding their children good-bye, talking about their next visit, or planning a Thanksgiving reunion. "I feel I am in India," she wrote. "Could this be the heartless America where family ties have lost their hold?"

Indians had it all wrong about the United States, my mother continued. She tried to explain why they read so much bad news about the country. "America is an open society as no other. So they expose their 'failings' too as no other," she wrote. "[Americans] cheerfully join in the talk of their own decline. But the decline is relative to America's own previous strength. It remains the world's largest economy; it still disposes of the greatest military might the world has known; refugees from terror still continue to seek shelter in this land of immigrants. It spends millions of dollars in the hope that someone, somewhere may make a valuable contribution to knowledge. America remains the yardstick by which we judge America." As you can see, she was hooked.

In those years, it was fashionable in elite Indian circles to denounce the United States for its imperialism and hegemony. During the Cold War, the Indian government routinely sided with the Soviet Union. Indira Gandhi, the populist prime minister, would often blame India's troubles on the "foreign hand," a reference to the CIA. But my mother has always been stubbornly pro-American. When my father was alive, he would sometimes criticize America for its crimes and blunders, partly to needle my brother and me and partly because, as one who had struggled for India's independence, he had absorbed the worldview of his closest allies, who were all on the left. Yet my mother remained unmoved, completely convinced that the United States was a land of amazing vitality and virtue. (I suspect it's what has helped her accept the fact that her sons chose the country as their home.)

Along with photographs and information brochures from her trip, my mother also brought back Harvard's course book. For me, it was an astonishing document. Instead of a thin pamphlet containing a dry list of subjects, as one would find at Indian universities, it was a bulging volume overflowing with ideas. It listed hundreds of classes in all kinds of fields. And the course descriptions were written like advertisements—as if the teachers wanted you to join them on an intellectual adventure. I read through the book, amazed that students didn't have to choose a major in advance and that they could take poetry and physics and history and economics. From eight thousand miles away, with little knowledge and no experience, I was falling in love with the idea of a liberal education.

I decided to follow in my brother's footsteps and
didn't pursue the Indian options available to me. I
took the SAT and wrote the required essays and applications. If you had asked me why I was so determined
to go to the United States, I couldn't have given you
a coherent response. Indian universities seemed limiting and limited. I thought about applying to British
universities, but I would have needed a scholarship
and few existed. The idea of "reading" just one subject
at Oxford or a narrow set of subjects at Cambridge
seemed less interesting when compared with the dazzling array of opportunities at the Ivy League schools.
And, of course, there was the allure of America.

I had always been fascinated by America. I had
visited once as a teenager, but most of my knowledge
about the country came from Hollywood. While the
Indian market was too poor and distant to get any
newly released movies, we watched the ones we would
get, a few years delayed—anything from *The Posei-
don Adventure* to *Kramer vs. Kramer*—as well as old
classics, like the Laurel and Hardy comedies, which
I loved. Television arrived in the country in the mid-
1970s, initially with just one government-run black-
and-white channel that mostly aired documentaries on
the glories of Indian agriculture. Every Sunday night,
my family would gather around the television set to

watch the one unadulterated piece of entertainment it would air, a Bollywood movie. Preceding that was a single episode of *I Love Lucy*, presumably all that Indian television could afford to import from the United States. Everyone watched it with pleasure, laughing along with Lucy and her crazy family. To this day, I have a soft spot for that show.

By the late 1970s, technology had begun to bring more of the West to India. A few of my friends had video recorders, and after a while, so did we. It was impossible to acquire actual copies of American movies and shows, but we did get many bootlegged versions. Somewhere in the United States, a relative would tape the latest television shows and send them to the family back home. These bootlegged Betamax tapes would be passed around in Bombay like samizdat publications in the Soviet Union.

The hottest show at the time was *Dallas*, which we all devoured. The scenes during the opening credits were my window into the American dream: shining shots of gleaming skyscrapers, helicopters landing in office parks, men in ten-gallon hats getting in and out of cavernous Cadillacs. And Victoria Principal—she was certainly part of my American dream. Whatever the newspapers said about problems in the United States, who could believe it with these images flashing across the screen? America seemed vast, energetic, and wealthy. Everything happened in Technicolor there.

The U.S. Information Service, set up to promote American culture and ideas during the Cold War, would hold screenings of older American classics. A friend and I would often attend these showings. There, in a small room in Bombay, sitting amid aging expats, I was introduced to Hollywood's golden age. I kept a scrapbook on these movies, from *It Happened One Night* to *Adam and Eve* to *How the West Was Won*. In a sense, they were my first real introduction to American history. And they added to my sense of the country as the world's most exciting place.

Let me be honest, though: while the soft attraction was great, so was the cold cash. My parents were well-paid professionals, but India was one of the poorest countries in the world. Their annual salaries combined would have equaled just half of one year's tuition abroad. At the time, American colleges did not offer need-blind admissions to foreign students like me—the schools all had much smaller endowments in those days—but they did distribute merit scholarships. And if you were admitted, they worked out a combination of grants, loans, and on-campus jobs that would allow you to attend. My brother's reports from Har-

vard were that between his scholarship and a campus job, he was making do quite well. He even had
enough money for books and incidental expenses. Yet
realizing that I needed not only admission but also a
scholarship added to my anxiety.

I got very lucky and ended up going to Yale. I have
no idea why they let me in or why I chose to go there.
I marvel today at college-bound American kids who
take two or three trips to campuses, sit in on classes,
have long discussions with counselors, and watch
student theater productions—all to decide where
to go to college. In comparison, I made an utterly
uninformed choice from halfway around the world. I
didn't get into Harvard, but I was fortunate to be able
to choose between Princeton and Yale and couldn't
really decide. I knew little about either. If I made a
list of each university's objective merits, which I did,
Princeton usually came out on top. It was smaller
and richer and had offered me a bigger scholarship.
Everyone had heard of it in India because of Albert
Einstein. Very few knew of Yale. This seems hard to
believe, but Yale really was quite obscure in India.
My father, like many Indians, couldn't pronounce
the name, and to his dying day he called it "Ale." In
general, American universities that have great name
recognition in India—and in Asia more generally—

are those with strong engineering programs, science departments, and business schools. These were not Yale's strengths.

Eventually, I decided to use the only mechanism I could think of: a coin toss. Heads, I would go to Yale; tails, I would go to Princeton. I flipped the coin. It was tails. So I decided to make it a "best of three" and tossed again. I don't remember if Yale won the coin toss at that point or if I kept going until it did. But in doing the exercise, I realized that I wanted to go to Yale. I don't quite know why. It is an example of the power of intuition. Though obviously both are great institutions, Yale was the perfect place for me. I knew something at the time that I couldn't explain or even understand.

Yale offered then, and still does now, a rigorous first-year academic program called Directed Studies. It is a sweeping survey of the Western literary and philosophical tradition from ancient Greece to modernity. This seemed like a wonderful opportunity for a kid from India. It would have introduced me to a number of great Western classics that I had heard about but never read. You had to apply to be able to take the courses, which I did. Some months later, I was thrilled to get a note informing me that I had been accepted into the program.

I chickened out. When I got to Yale, it was time for me to finalize my choices. I tallied up the subjects that I believed I *had* to take—courses like math, computer programming, and physics—and realized that if I were going to enroll in Directed Studies, it would fill up most of my schedule. I panicked at the idea of committing so completely to something that seemed so impractical. I remember thinking to myself, "When people ask me in India over the summer about my courses, I could talk about computers and math. How would I explain *this*?" So I dropped Directed Studies and signed up for courses that seemed more sensible.

In my first year, however, I allowed myself to pick one class simply out of sheer interest. The course was a popular lecture on the history of the Cold War, taught by a political science professor named H. Bradford Westerfield. His lectures were packed with vivid details and delivered with gusto. I was hooked.

International politics and economics had always appealed to me. As a teenager in India, I would avidly read the major international newspapers and magazines, which sometimes arrived weeks after they were published. The great global drama of the times was the clash of the superpowers, and it echoed in India, a country that was torn between the two camps. I remember devouring the excerpts of Henry Kissinger's memoirs when they came out, though I'm sure I didn't understand them. (I was fifteen at the time.) Yet I never thought that one studied these kinds of subjects in college. I had assumed that I would major in something that was practical, technical, and job oriented. I could always read newspapers on the side. Westerfield's course, however, made me realize that I should take my passion seriously, even without being sure what it might lead to in terms of a profession. That spring, I declared my major in history. I was going to get a liberal education.

But still, I couldn't have answered the question, what is a liberal education?

2

A Brief History of
Liberal Education

FOR MOST OF human history, education was job training. Hunters, farmers, and warriors taught the young to hunt, farm, and fight. Children of the ruling class received instruction in the arts of war and governance, but this too was intended first and foremost as preparation for the roles they would assume later in society, not for any broader purpose. All that began to change twenty-five hundred years ago in ancient Greece.

Prior to the change, education in Greece had centered on the development of *arête*, roughly meaning excellence or virtue. The scholar Bruce Kimball notes that the course of study largely involved the memorization and recitation of Homeric epic poetry.* Through immersion in the world of gods and goddesses, kings and warriors, children would master the Greek language and imbibe the lessons, codes, and values considered important by the ruling elite. Physical training was a crucial element of Greek education. In the city-state of Sparta, the most extreme example of this focus, young boys considered weak at birth were abandoned to die. The rest were sent to grueling boot camps, where they were toughened into Spartan soldiers from an early age.

Around the fifth century BC, some Greek city-states, most notably Athens, began to experiment with a new form of government. "Our constitution is called a democracy," the Athenian statesman Pericles noted in his funeral oration, "because power is in the hands not of a minority but of the whole people." This innovation in government required a simultaneous innovation in education. Basic skills for sustenance were no longer sufficient—citizens also had to be properly trained to run their own society. The link between

---

* Bruce Kimball, *Orators and Philosophers: A History of the Idea of Liberal Education* (New York: Teachers College Press, 1986), is especially enlightening on ancient and early education, and I draw on it, among other sources, for the paragraphs dealing with that period.

a broad education and liberty became important to the Greeks. Describing this approach to instruction centuries later, the Romans coined a term for it: a "liberal" education, using the word *liberal* in its original Latin sense, "of or pertaining to free men." More than two thousand years later, Frederick Douglass saw the same connection. When his master heard that young Frederick was reading well, he was furious, saying, "Learning will spoil the best nigger in the world. If he learns to read the Bible it will forever unfit him to be a slave." Douglass recalled that he "instinctively assented to the proposition, and from that moment I understood the direct pathway from slavery to freedom."

From the beginning, people disagreed over the purpose of a liberal education. (Perhaps intellectual disagreement is inherent in the idea itself.) The first great divide took place in ancient Greece, between Plato, the philosopher, and Isocrates, the orator. Plato and his followers, including Aristotle, considered education a search for truth. Inspired by Socrates, they used the dialectic mode of reasoning and discourse to pursue knowledge in its purest form. Isocrates, on the other hand, hearkened back to the tradition of *arête*. He and his followers believed a person could best arrive at virtue and make a good living by studying the arts of rhetoric, language, and morality. This debate—between those who understand liberal education in instrumental terms and those who see it as an end in and of itself—has continued to the present day.

In general, the more practical rationale for liberal education gained the upper hand in the ancient world. Yet the two traditions have never been mutually exclusive. The Roman statesman and philosopher Cicero, one of the earliest writers on record to use the term *artes liberales*, wanted to combine the search for truth with rhetoric, which was seen as a more useful skill. "For it is from knowledge that oratory must derive its beauty and fullness," the philosopher-statesman wrote around 55 BC. While debate continues, the reality is that liberal education has always combined a mixture of both approaches—practical and philosophical.

Science was central to liberal education from the start. Except that in those days, the reason to study it was the precise opposite of what is argued today. In the ancient world, and for many centuries thereafter, science was seen as a path to abstract knowledge. It had no practical purpose. Humanistic subjects, like language and history, on the other hand, equipped the young to function well in the world as politicians, courtiers, lawyers, and merchants. And yet the Greeks and Romans studied geometry and astronomy alongside rhetoric and grammar. In the first century BC, this dualistic approach to education was "finally and definitively formalized" into a system described as "the seven liberal arts." The curriculum was split between science and humanities, the theoretical and the practical. Centuries later, it was often divided into two subgroups: the trivium—grammar, logic, and rhetoric—was taught first; the quadrivium—arithmetic, geometry, music, and astronomy—came next.

Soldiers and statesmen, naturally, placed greater emphasis on subjects they thought of as practical—what today we would call the humanities. But even so, the idea of a broader education always persisted. In the eighth century, Charlemagne, king of the Franks (a Germanic tribe that inhabited large chunks of present-day Germany, France, Belgium, Netherlands, and Luxembourg), consolidated his empire. Bruce Kimball notes that Charlemagne then established a palace school and named as its master Alcuin, an English scholar (even then Englishmen were the ideal headmasters). Alcuin and his followers concentrated on grammar and textual analysis and demoted mathematics, but they continued to teach some version of the liberal arts. And the deeper quest for understanding never disappeared. Even during the Dark Ages, medieval monasteries kept alive a tradition of learning and inquiry.

Why did European learning move beyond monasteries? One influence might have been Islam, the most advanced civilization in the Middle Ages—something difficult to imagine today. Within the world of Islam there were dozens of madrasas—schools where history, politics, science, music, and many other subjects were studied and where research was pursued (though not all Islamic educational institutions were called madrasas). Islamic learning produced innovations, especially in the study of mathematics. Algebra comes from the Arab phrase *al-jabr*, meaning "the reunion of broken parts." The name of the Persian scholar al-Khwārizmī was translated into Latin as *algoritmi*, which became "algorithm." By the eleventh century, Cairo's al-Azhar and Baghdad's Nizamiyah were famous across the world for their academic accomplishments, as were many other centers of learning in the Arab world. This Islamic influence found a home in the Muslim regions of continental Europe as well, in the madrasas of Moorish Spain, in Granada, Córdoba, Seville, and elsewhere.

By the late Middle Ages, Europe's stagnation was ending. The expansion in global trade and travel meant that its leaders needed greater knowledge and expertise in areas like geography, law, and science. As city-states competed with one another economically, they sought out individuals with better skills and education. Because of its long coastline, Italy became a place where commerce, trade, and capitalism were beginning to stir. Groups of scholars started coming together in various Italian cities to study theology, canon and civil law, and other subjects. These scholars came from great distances and were often grouped by their geographical origins, each one being called a "nation," an early use of the word. Some of these "nations" hired local scholars, administered exams, and joined together into groups that came to be called *universitas*. These organizations sought and were granted special protections from local laws, thus allowing them necessary freedoms and autonomy.

In 1088, Europe's first university was founded in Bologna. Over the next century, similar institutions sprouted up in Paris, Oxford, Cambridge, and Padua. By 1300, western Europe was home to between fifteen and twenty universities. These schools were initially not bastions of free inquiry, but they did become places where scholars discussed some taboo subjects, recovered, translated, and studied Aristotle's writings, and subjected laws to close scrutiny. Yet most research took place outside of universities in those days because of their religious influence. It was heretical, for instance, for scientists to speculate on earth's place amid the stars. In most cities, while students were accorded some of the same freedoms and exemptions as the clergy, they desired even more. The University of Padua's motto was *Universa universis patavina libertas*—"Paduan freedom is universal for everyone."

In the fourteenth century, the balance between practical and philosophical knowledge shifted again. Some Italian scholars and writers believed that universities had become too specialized. They looked to return European education to its Greek and Roman roots. These humanists rejected the highly detailed, scholastic approach to learning and theology that was pervasive in medieval universities. Instead, as the late scholar Paul Oskar Kristeller notes, they encouraged a "revival of arts and of letters, of eloquence and of learning" that "led to a new and intensified study of ancient literature and history." Over the next two centuries, what has been called Renaissance humanism spread to the rest of Europe.

These traditions of scholarship, however, did not create the experience we now think of as a liberal education. That modern tradition had less to do with universities and more with colleges. And "college as we know it," writes Columbia University professor Andrew Delbanco, "is a fundamentally English idea."* The earliest English colleges were founded in the thirteenth century for scholars of divinity whose duties, Delbanco notes, "included celebrating mass for the soul of the benefactor who had endowed the college and thereby spared them from menial work." Religious influences were strong—the public lecture, for instance, was a secular outgrowth of the Sunday sermon—though the curriculum was varied and included non-theological subjects.

Colleges grew more secular by the nineteenth century as seminaries assumed responsibility for training ministers. They also began to develop a character distinct from European universities, which were becoming increasingly focused on research, especially in Germany. Unlike universities, which often lacked a clear physical embodiment, colleges were defined by their architecture. An imposing stone building was usually constructed with an open courtyard in the center and student dormitories arrayed around it. The "common" room was where students could meet, the chapel where they could pray, and the library where they could read. This model of a

---

* I draw on Delbanco's excellent book *College: What It Was, Is, and Should Be* (Princeton, NJ: Princeton University Press, 2012), among others, for the early years of American higher education.

residential college originated in England and spread to the Anglo-American world, where it remains the distinctive form for undergraduates.

In the early twentieth century, among the major universities, Harvard and Yale adopted the full-fledged residential college model for student housing, partly in an effort to retain the intimate setting of liberal arts colleges while pursuing their ambitions to become great research universities. The residential college has come to be seen as possessing certain qualities that enhance the experience of liberal education beyond the curriculum. The advantages of such an arrangement are often described today in terms like "living-learning experiences," "peer-to-peer education," and "lateral learning." Samuel Eliot Morison, the legendary historian of Harvard, best described the distinctive benefits of the residential setting: "Book learning alone might be got by lectures and reading; but it was only by studying and disputing, eating and drinking, playing and praying as members of the same collegiate community, in close and constant association with each other and with their tutors, that the priceless gift of character could be imparted." An emphasis on building character, stemming from the religious origins of colleges, remains an aim of liberal arts colleges almost everywhere, at least in theory.

America's earliest colleges were modeled on their English predecessors. Many of the founders of Harvard College, for example, were graduates of Emmanuel College at Cambridge University. Perhaps because, in America, they did not start out strictly as seminaries, colonial colleges often incorporated into their curricula a variety of disciplines, including the sciences, humanities, and law. Students were expected to take all these subjects and relate them to one another because it was assumed there was a single, divine intelligence behind all of them. In Cardinal John Newman's nineteenth-century formulation of this approach to education, "The subject-matter of knowledge is intimately united in itself, as being the acts and the work of the Creator." It was a theological version of what physicists today call the unified field theory.

America's first colleges stuck to curricula that could be described as God and Greeks—theology and classics. But a great debate over this approach emerged at the beginning of the nineteenth century. People wondered why students should be required to study ancient Greek and Latin. They suggested that colleges should begin to incorporate modern languages and subjects into their instruction. After all, the country was growing rapidly and developing economically and technologically, making the college course of study seem antiquated in comparison. After much deliberation, the Yale faculty issued a report in 1828 defending the classical curriculum. It powerfully influenced American colleges for half a century—delaying, some might say, their inevitable evolution. It also, however, outlined a central tension in liberal education that persists till now.

The Yale report explained that the essence of liberal education was "not to teach that which is peculiar to any one of the professions; but to lay the foundation which is common to them all." It described its two goals in terms that still resonate: training the mind to think and filling the mind with specific content.

The two great points to be gained in intellectual culture, are the discipline and the furniture of the mind; expanding its powers, and storing it with knowledge. The former of these is, perhaps, the more important of the two. A commanding object, therefore, in a collegiate course, should be, to call into daily and vigorous exercise the faculties of the student. Those branches of study should be prescribed, and those modes of instruction adopted, which are best calculated to teach the art of fixing the attention, directing the train of thought, analyzing a subject proposed for investigation; follow-

ing, with accurate discrimination, the course of argument; balancing nicely the evidence presented to the
judgment; awakening, elevating, and controlling the
imagination; arranging, with skill, the treasures which
memory gathers; rousing and guiding the powers of
genius.

Though its particular aim historically was to
defend the classical curriculum, the Yale report's
broader argument was that learning to think is more
important than the specific topics and books that
are taught. A Harvard man revived the argument
fifty years later, as he battled to undo the report's
recommendations.

Charles Eliot was an unlikely candidate for the
presidency of Harvard. He was a scientist at a time
when the heads of schools like Harvard, Yale, and
Princeton were still generally ministers. After grad-
uating from Harvard in 1853, Eliot was appointed
to be a tutor and later an assistant professor of mathematics and chemistry at the school. But he was
not made a full professor as he had hoped, and at
about the same time, his bad luck compounded as his
father's fortune collapsed. Eliot decided to travel to
Europe, where he saw firsthand the rapidly changing state of higher education on the Continent and

the rise of the great research universities in Germany. He then returned to the United States to take up a professorship at the Massachusetts Institute of Technology in 1865. At the time, like many other colleges, Harvard was in the midst of a tumultuous period in its history. It faced calls for more vocational education in order to prepare Americans for the workforce in the rapidly industrializing economy just emerging from the Civil War.

To address these concerns, Eliot penned a two-part essay in the *Atlantic Monthly* titled "The New Education." It began with words that could be uttered by any parent today, adjusted for gender: "What can I do with my boy? I can afford, and am glad, to give him the best training to be had. I should be proud to have him turn out a preacher or a learned man; but I don't think he has the making of that in him. I want to give him a practical education; one that will prepare him, better than I was prepared, to follow my business or any other active calling." Eliot's answer was that Americans needed to combine the best developments of the emerging European research university with the best traditions of the classic American college.

Eliot proposed that America's great universities embrace the research function, but that they do so at the graduate level, leaving undergraduates free to explore their interests more broadly. He showed a strong understanding and mastery of the emerging trends in education, like the difference between scientific and humanistic fields and the rise in technical training. He wanted colleges to distinguish carefully between a skills-based and a liberal education, the latter of which he considered more important. Months after his essays were published, at the age of thirty-five, Charles Eliot was offered the presidency of Harvard, a post that he held for four decades—exactly—and from which he reshaped the university and the country.

Eliot made so many transforming changes at Harvard that they are impossible to recount—he essentially established the modern American university. Yet perhaps his most influential reform, at least for undergraduates, was his advocacy for a curriculum based on the "spontaneous diversity of choice." In other words, under his new system, students had very few required courses and many electives. Previously in American colleges, much of the curriculum had been set in stone. Students had enrolled in courses and studied topics in a predetermined sequence from one year to the next. The faculty had believed, in the terms of the Yale report, that it should choose "the furniture" that was to inhabit the students' minds.

Eliot disagreed profoundly. He was probably influenced by his Protestantism, which saw the individual as the best mediator of his own fate. But perhaps more than anything, he was imbued with the spirit of Ralph Waldo Emerson and his distinctively American ideas, which were deeply influential at the time. For Emerson, the task of every human being was to find his or her voice and give expression to it. "Trust thyself," Emerson wrote in "Self-Reliance." "Every heart vibrates to that iron string." Emerson's notion of the importance of authenticity, as opposed to imitation, and his praise of unique thinking could have been turned into copy for Apple ad campaigns ("Think Different").

In an 1885 speech, Eliot outlined the case for his elective system using language that remains radical today—and with which many parents might still disagree. "At eighteen the American boy has passed the age when a compulsory external discipline is useful," Eliot wrote. "A well-instructed youth of eighteen can select for himself—not for any other boy, or for the fictitious universal boy but for himself alone—a better course of study than any college faculty, or any wise man who does not know him and his ancestors and his previous life, can possibly select for him." Eliot believed that American liberal education should allow you to choose your own courses, excite your own imagination, and thus realize your distinctive self. Many responded that some subjects are not worthy of being taught. The solution, he believed, was to let faculty members offer what they want and students to take what they like.

Eliot's views were not shared by many influential educators of the time, most notably the president of Princeton, James McCosh. (In fact, Eliot's speech that I quote from above was from a public debate with McCosh on the topic in New York City.) A Scottish minister and philosopher, McCosh thought that universities should provide a specific framework of learning and a hierarchy of subjects for their students—or else they were failing in their role as guardians. In particular, religion could not simply be treated like any other subject, to be taken or dropped at an undergraduate's whim. Eliot's ideas, however, were more in sync with American culture and its emphasis on individualism and freedom of choice. Over time, the elective system in some form or another has come to dominate American higher education, with a few notable exceptions.

In the early years of the twentieth century, a swell in the tide of immigrants entering the United States prompted concern among some citizens, educators, and public officials that the country was losing its character. Against that backdrop, an English professor at Columbia University, John Erskine, began offering a two-year course called General Honors in 1920. Erskine "wanted to provide young people from different backgrounds with a common culture, something he thought was already thin in the United States," writes the Harvard scholar Louis Menand. Erskine believed that the best way to become truly educated was to immerse oneself in great works of the past.

In 1930, Mortimer Adler, an educator who had taught a section in Erskine's program, left Columbia for the University of Chicago. His friend Robert Maynard Hutchins had recently been appointed president of the school, and the two began teaching a seminar together for underclassmen on classic works in the Western canon. The course evolved into a "great books" program—a core curriculum in which students read prescribed works of history, literature, and philosophy and then gather for small-group discussions guided by faculty members. Several years later, two professors named Stringfellow Barr and Scott Buchanan moved from Chicago to St. John's College in Annapolis to start their own great-books program. Barr and Buchanan radically altered the undergraduate curriculum at the small school with the tradition of seven liberal arts in mind. Even science was taught from a great-books perspective, reading classic accounts that were, in many ways, outdated or had been superseded. The program left no room for electives.

By the 1930s and 1940s—perhaps because the immigrant tide had receded with the introduction of national quotas in 1921 and 1924—interest in the common core waned. Today, about 150 schools in the United States offer some kind of core program based on great books, though very few require that all undergraduates take it, as Columbia, Chicago, and St. John's do.

Whatever its merits, the idea of a curriculum based on some set of great books has always been debated. In a 1952 essay, Hutchins, who could be considered the father of the great-books movement, made what has become a familiar case for it. "Until lately the West has regarded it as self-evident that the road to education lay through great books," Hutchins wrote. "No man was educated unless he was acquainted with the masterpieces of his tradition." Times have changed, but political and social changes cannot "invalidate the tradition or make it irrelevant for modern men," he insisted. Except that, as we have seen, this account is not entirely true. Everyone who has ever set up a great-books program based it on the belief that, in the good old days, people used to study a set of agreed-upon classics. In fact, from the start of liberal education, there were disputes over what men (and women) should read and how much or how little freedom they should have to follow their curiosity. Martha Nussbaum, a philosopher at the University of Chicago, argues that the Socratic tradition of inquiry by its nature rejected an approach dependent "on canonical texts that had moral authority." She writes, "It is an irony of the contemporary 'culture wars' that the Greeks are frequently brought onstage as heroes in the 'great books' curricula proposed by many conservatives. For there is nothing on which the Greek philosophers were more eloquent, and more unanimous, than the limitations of such curricula."

I've found that my own views on this subject have changed over time, from my days as an undergraduate, then as a teacher in graduate school, and now as a parent. In college, I was attracted to the idea of a common core—though I didn't end up studying one. And yet I wished I had more of a grounding in some areas, and found myself playing catch-up. When teaching undergraduates in the 1980s, I was struck not only by how bright they were but also by how little they knew about, say, the basic outlines of American history. They could analyze everything placed in front of them, but if you asked them to put six events in chronological order, they would get many of them wrong. I thought it would be worthwhile to require exposure to a set of facts or books—furniture for the mind—that would give students a foundation from which to then roam freely. And they had room to roam. Remember, most advocates of a core do not consider it sufficient for a liberal education. The programs at Columbia and Chicago allow for many electives. Proportionally, the core represents only a part of the overall curriculum.

There are also social benefits to a common core. All students are able to share an intellectual experience. They can discuss it together, join in its delights, and commiserate over its weaknesses. It's ultimately a bonding opportunity. "Once they have gone through the Core," writes Delbanco, referring to Columbia's program specifically, "no student is a complete stranger to any other." That sense of being part of a larger group becomes even more useful later in life, when one is expected to work with one's peers and colleagues toward common goals in a professional setting. As campuses get more diverse and students spend time pursuing more narrowly focused studies and highly targeted extracurricular activities, something needs to define the collective educational experience.

I still sympathize with arguments in support of a

core, but I have come to place a greater value than I once did on the openness inherent in liberal education—the ability for the mind to range widely and pursue interests freely. In my own experience, the courses I took simply because I felt I needed to know some subject matter or acquire cultural literacy have faded in my memory. Those that I took out of genuine curiosity or because I was inspired by a great teacher have left a more lasting and powerful impression. After all, one can always read a book to get the basic information about a particular topic, or simply use Google. The crucial challenge is to learn how to read critically, analyze data, and formulate ideas—and most of all to enjoy the intellectual adventure enough to be able to do them easily and often.

Loving to learn is a greater challenge today than it used to be. I've watched my children grow up surrounded by an amazing cornucopia of entertainment available instantly on their computers, tablets, and phones. Perhaps soon these pleasures will be hardwired into their brains. The richness, variety, and allure of today's games, television shows, and videos are dazzling. Many are amazingly creative, and some are intellectually challenging—there are smart video games out there. But all are designed to get children enraptured and, eventually, addicted. The all-consuming power of modern entertainment can turn something that demands active and sustained engagement, like reading and writing, into a chore.

And yet reading—especially, I would argue, reading books—remains one of the most important paths to real knowledge. There are few substitutes to understanding an issue in depth than reading a good book about it. This has been true for centuries, and it has not changed. And kids need to enjoy reading— not just see it as the thing their parents make them do before they can play video games or watch a television show. If having teenagers read Philip Roth's *Goodbye, Columbus* rather than Jane Austen's novels makes this more likely, so be it. I don't decry or condemn new forms of entertainment and technology. They open up new vistas of knowledge and ways of thinking. Our children will be smarter and quicker than us in many ways. But a good education system must confront the realities of the world we live in and educate in a way that addresses them, rather than pretend that these challenges don't exist.

And then there are those strange college courses on, say, "transgendered roles in East-African poetry" that infuriate conservative critics of higher education. They are right to be dismayed at the bizarre and narrow content, but it comes about for reasons that are often nonpolitical. Some of the most controversial features of modern liberal education have come into being not out of intellectual conviction but from bureaucratic convenience. As America's best colleges became the world's best universities, the imperatives of the latter began to dominate the former. Research has trumped teaching in most large universities—no one gets tenure for teaching. But as important, the curriculum has also been warped to satisfy research. Professors find that it is dreary and laborious for them to teach basic courses that might be interesting and useful for students. It is much easier to offer seminars on their current research interests, no matter how small, obscure, or irrelevant the topic is to undergraduates. As knowledge becomes more specialized, the courses offered to students become more arcane. It is this impulse that produces the seemingly absurd courses one finds in some colleges today, as much as the subversive desires of a left-wing professoriat.

Another development, again unrelated to any intellectual theory about liberal education, has been the abandonment of rigor, largely in the humanities. Grades have risen steadily in almost all American colleges in recent decades. Today, 43 percent of all grades awarded are in the A range—up from 15 percent in 1960. This is an outgrowth of a complex set of factors, one of which is indeed the rising quality of students. But others are bureaucratic and philosophical, such as the 1960s assault on hierarchy. I can attest from personal experience that handing out high marks can be convenient for faculty interests. When I was a teaching assistant at Harvard, I quickly realized that giving B minuses or below meant that the students would come to complain at length; ask you to reconsider, maybe give them another chance to do the work over; and even raise the issue with their advisor or a dean. It meant lots of work for me. The much easier strategy was to give everyone a B plus or an A minus, reserving the straight A for works of genuine distinction. (I tried to resist but was certainly guilty of taking the easy way out more than once.) I cannot say if the incentives remain the same, but I notice that the portion of all grades that are A or A minus at Harvard has risen from a third (in 1986) to a half (in 2006). And the most commonly awarded grade at Harvard today is a straight A—not even an A minus.

The greatest shift in liberal education over the past century has been the downgrading of subjects in science and technology. Historically, beginning with Greek and Roman developments in education, scientific exploration was pursued through the lens of "natural philosophy." In the Middle Ages, the subject was seen as part of an effort to explain God's creation and man's role within it. But during the age of scientific revolutions, and coming to a climax in the nineteenth century with Charles Darwin's theory of evolution, the study of science increasingly conflicted with religion. This led to the discipline losing its central position in liberal education, which was still then grounded in a pious outlook that sought to understand not only the mystery of life but also its purpose. As Anthony Kronman writes, a rise in scientific research meant "a material universe whose structure could now be described with astounding precision but which was itself devoid of meaning and purpose. As a result, the physical sciences ceased to be concerned with, or to have much to contribute to, the search for an answer to the question of the meaning of life." Science was relegated to scientists—a huge loss to society as a whole.

By the middle of the twentieth century, following the quantum revolution in physics, laypeople found it even more difficult to understand science and integrate it into other fields of knowledge. In 1959, C. P. Snow, an English physicist and novelist, wrote a famous essay, "The Two Cultures," in which he warned that the polarization of knowledge into two camps was producing "mutual incomprehension . . . hostility and dislike." He explains:

A good many times I have been present at gatherings
of people who, by the standards of the traditional culture, are thought highly educated and who have with
considerable gusto been expressing their incredulity at
the illiteracy of scientists. Once or twice I have been
provoked and have asked the company how many of
them could describe the Second Law of Thermody-
namics. The response was cold: it was also negative.
Yet I was asking something which is about the scientific equivalent of: Have you read a work of Shake-
speare's? I now believe that if I had asked an even
simpler question—such as, What do you mean by
mass, or acceleration, which is the scientific equivalent
of saying, Can you read?—not more than one in ten of
the highly educated would have felt that I was speaking the same language. So the great edifice of modern
physics goes up, and the majority of the cleverest people in the western world have about as much insight
into it as their neolithic ancestors would have had.

In 2003, Lawrence Summers, then president of Harvard, echoed Snow's concerns and advocated a return
to scientific literacy for all at the undergraduate level.
Former Princeton president Shirley Tilghman, herself a scientist, argued in 2010 that discussions of
public policy are impoverished because of the basic

ignorance of science that pervades American society today. Nonscientists need to understand science, she contends, and scientists are best off with a strong background in other subjects as well. And yet little has changed on this front in recent years.

The most interesting and ambitious effort to reform liberal education for the twenty-first century is not taking place in America. In fact, it is taking place about as far away from the United States as one can possibly get—Singapore. In 2011, Yale University joined with the National University of Singapore to establish a new liberal arts school in Asia called Yale-NUS College, and in the fall of 2013, it welcomed its first class of 157 students from twenty-six countries. When I was a trustee at Yale, I enthusiastically supported this venture. The project—though not without risks—has the potential to create a beachhead for broad-based liberal education in a part of the world that, while rising to the center stage globally, remains relentlessly focused on skills-based instruction.

Scholars from both universities have used the venture as an opportunity to reexamine the concept of liberal education in an increasingly connected and globalized world. The curriculum of Yale-NUS reflects that thinking, in some parts drawing on the best of the old tradition, in some parts refining it, and in some parts creating a whole new set of ideas about teaching the young. In April 2013, a committee of this new enterprise set forth the ideas that will define the college. It is an extraordinary document and, if implemented well, could serve as a model for the liberal arts college of the future.

The Yale-NUS report is radical and innovative. First, the school calls itself a college of liberal arts *and sciences*, to restore science to its fundamental place in an undergraduate's education. It abolishes departments, seeing them as silos that inhibit cross-fertilization, interdisciplinary works, and synergy. It embraces a core curriculum, which takes up most of the first two years of study but is very different from the Columbia-Chicago model. The focus of the Yale-NUS core is to expose students to a variety of modes of thinking. In one module they are to learn how experimental scientists conduct research; in another, how statistics informs social science and public policy. There is a strong emphasis throughout on exposing students to scientific methods rather than scientific facts so that—whatever their ultimate major—they are aware of the way in which science works.

The Yale-NUS core does include courses on the great books, but it does not treat them as simply a canon to be checked off on a cultural literacy list.

The books selected are viewed as interesting examples of a genre, chosen not because they are part of a "required" body of knowledge but because they benefit from careful analysis. The emphasis again is on the method of inquiry. Students learn how to read, unpack, and then write about a great work of literature or philosophy or art. The curriculum requires students to take on projects outside the classroom, in the belief that a "work" component teaches valuable lessons that learning from a book cannot. This part has a powerful practical appeal. I once asked Jeff Bewkes, the CEO of Time Warner, what skill was most useful in business that wasn't taught in college or graduate schools. He immediately replied, "Teamwork. You have to know how to work with people and get others to want to work with you. It's probably the crucial skill, and yet education is mostly about solo performances."

The greatest innovation in the Yale-NUS curriculum comes directly from the nature of the association between the two universities and their home cultures. Students study not only Plato and Aristotle but also, in the same course, Confucius and the Buddha—and ask why their systems of ethics might be similar or different. They study the *Odyssey* and the *Ramayana*. They examine the "primitivisms" of Paul Gauguin and Pablo Picasso while also looking at the woodcarvings from the South Sea Islands and the ukiyo-e tradition of Japanese woodblock prints that influenced Western artists. And, of course, as they study modern history, politics, and economics, they will naturally find themselves taking a more comparative approach to the topics than any college in the United States or Asia would likely do by itself. Multiculturalism in education is usually a cliché that indicates little of substance, or involves Western critiques of the West (like those of the writer Frantz Fanon or the historian Howard Zinn). The Yale-NUS curriculum is built to provide a genuine multicultural education in a college designed for the emerging multicultural world. In studying other societies, students learn much more about their own. It is only by having some point of comparison that one can understand the distinctive qualities of Western or Chinese or Indian culture.

Yale-NUS is in its very early days. It may not be able to implement all its ideas. It does not solve all the problems of a liberal education. The tensions between freedom of inquiry and the still-closed political system in Singapore might undermine the project. But the educators involved have conceived of the college's mission and mandate brilliantly, and have pointed the way to a revived, rigorous liberal education that recovers the importance of science, places teaching at its heart, combines a core with open exploration, and reflects the direction the world is headed, in which knowledge of new countries and cultures is an essential component of any education. Yale-NUS should become a model studied around the world.

But what if a liberal education done well still doesn't get you a job? In 1852, Cardinal Newman wrote that a student of liberal education "apprehends the great outlines of knowledge" for its own sake rather than to acquire skills to practice a trade or do a job. Even then, he noted, there were skeptics who raised questions of practicality. As we have seen, such questions have surrounded the idea of liberal education since the days of Isocrates, and they persist today. Newman tells us that his critics would ask him, "To what then does it lead? where does it end? what does it do? How does it profit?" Or as a former president of Yale, the late A. Bartlett Giamatti, put it in one of his beautiful lectures, "What is the earthly use of all this kind of education?"

So, what *is* the earthly use of a liberal education?

3

Learning to Think

WHEN YOU HEAR someone extol the benefits of a liberal education, you will probably hear him or her say that "it teaches you how to think." I'm sure that's true. But for me, the central virtue of a liberal education is that it teaches you how to write, and writing makes you think. Whatever you do in life, the ability to write clearly, cleanly, and reasonably quickly will prove to be an invaluable skill.

In my freshman year of college, I took an English composition course. My teacher, an elderly Englishman with a sharp wit and an even sharper red pencil, was a tough grader. He would return my essays with dozens of comments written in the margins, each one highlighting something that was vague or confusing or poorly articulated. I realized that in coming from India, I was pretty good at taking tests and regurgitating things I had memorized; I was not so good at expressing my own ideas. By the time I got to college, I had taken many, many exams but written almost no papers. That was not unusual even at a good high school in Asia in the 1970s, and it's still true in many places there today.

Over the course of that semester, I found myself starting to make the connection between my thoughts and words. It was hard. Being forced to write clearly means, first, you have to think clearly. I began to recognize that the two processes are inextricably intertwined. In what is probably an apocryphal story, when the columnist Walter Lippmann was once asked his views on a particular topic, he is said to have replied, "I don't know what I think on that one. I haven't written about it yet."

In modern philosophy, there is a great debate as to which comes first—thought or language. Do we think abstractly and then put those ideas into words, or do we think in words that then create a scaffolding of thought? I can speak only from my own experience. When I begin to write, I realize that my "thoughts" are usually a jumble of half-formed ideas strung together, with gaping holes between them. It is the act of writing that forces me to sort them out. Writing the first draft of a column or an essay is an expression of self-knowledge—learning just what I think about a topic, whether there is a logical sequence to my ideas, and whether the conclusion flows from the facts at hand. No matter who you are—a politician, a businessperson, a lawyer, a historian, or a novelist—writing forces you to make choices and brings clarity and order to your ideas.

If you think this has no earthly use, ask Jeff Bezos, the founder of Amazon. Bezos insists that his senior executives write memos, often as long as six printed pages, and begins senior-management meetings with a period of quiet time, sometimes as long as thirty minutes, while everyone reads the "narratives" to themselves and makes notes on them. If proposing a new product or strategy, the memo must take the form of a press release, using simple, jargon-free language so that a layperson can understand it. In an interview with *Fortune*'s Adam Lashinsky, Bezos said, "Full sentences are harder to write. They have verbs. The paragraphs have topic sentences. There is no way to write a six-page, narratively structured memo and not have clear thinking."

Norman Augustine, reflecting on his years as the CEO of Lockheed Martin, recalled that "the firm I led at the end of my formal business career employed some one hundred eighty thousand people, mostly college graduates, of whom over eighty thousand were engineers or scientists. I have concluded that one of the stronger correlations with advancement through the management ranks was the ability of an individual to express clearly his or her thoughts in writing."

The second great advantage of a liberal education is that it teaches you how to speak. The Yale-NUS report states that the college wants to make "articulate communication" central to its intellectual experience. That involves writing, of course, but also the ability to give compelling verbal explanations of, say, scientific experiments or to deliver presentations before small and large groups. At the deepest level, articulate communication helps you to speak your mind. This doesn't mean spouting anything and everything you're thinking at any given moment. It means learning to understand your own mind, to filter out under-developed ideas, and then to express to the outside world your thoughts, arranged in some logical order.

Another difference that struck me between school in India and college in the United States was that talking was an important component of my grade. My professors were going to judge me on my ability to think through the subject matter and to present my analysis and conclusions—out loud. The seminar, a form of teaching and learning at the heart of liberal education, helps you to read, analyze, and dissect. Above all, it helps you to express yourself. And this emphasis on "articulate communication" is reinforced in the many extracurricular activities that surround every liberal arts college—theater, debate, political unions, student government, protest groups. In order to be successful in life, you often have to gain your peers' attention and convince them of your cause, sometimes in a five-minute elevator pitch.

The study and practice of speech actually figured far more prominently in the early centuries of liberal education. Rhetoric was among the most important subjects taught—often *the* most important. It was intimately connected not only with philosophy but also with governance and action. In the centuries before print, oral communication was at the center of public and professional life. The eighteenth- and nineteenth-century college curricula in Britain and the United States maintained that emphasis on oratory.

In the twentieth century, as research became the major focus of large universities, and the printed text became the dominant method of mass communication, the emphasis on speech faded, especially in the United States. In Great Britain, public speaking remains prominent in a tradition of poetry recitation and elocution, debate and declamation. At the center of Britain's political life stands the House of Commons, a venue in which the ability to thrust and parry verbally gains a politician notice by his or her peers. That's why so many Britons sound intelligent, lucid, and witty—it's not just the accent. The rise of television and digital video have made verbal fluency useful, sometimes crucial. Whether for public or private communication, the ability to articulate your thoughts clearly will prove to be a tremendous strength. No matter how strong your idea, you have to be able to convince others to get behind it.

A related method of learning through the ages has been something that is often thought of as pure pleasure—conversation. "Conversation," a former president of Yale, A. Whitney Griswold, wrote, "is the oldest form of instruction of the human race," defining it as "the great creative art whereby man translates feeling into reason and shares with his fellow man those innermost thoughts and ideals of which civilization is made." The scientist and philosopher Alfred North Whitehead once confessed that "outside of the book-knowledge which is necessary to our professional training, I think I got most of my development from the good conversation to which I have always had the luck to have access." This is probably the insight behind the "open-plan office" that encourages meetings, chats, and conversation throughout the workday. For my part, I have found that interviewing people, exchanging views with peers and friends, and arguing at editorial meetings have been crucial to learning.

That brings me to the third great strength of a liberal education: it teaches you how to learn. I now realize that what I gained from college and graduate school, far more lasting than any specific set of facts or piece of knowledge, has been the understanding of how to acquire knowledge on my own. I learned how to read an essay closely, search for new sources, find data to prove or disprove a hypothesis, and detect an author's prejudices. I learned how to read a book fast and still get its essence. I learned to ask questions, present an opposing view, take notes, and, nowadays, watch speeches, lectures, and interviews as they stream across my computer. And most of all, I learned that learning was a pleasure—a great adventure of exploration.

Whatever job you take, the specific subjects you studied in college will probably prove somewhat irrelevant to the day-to-day work you will do soon after you graduate. And even if they are relevant, that will change. People who learned to write code for computers just ten years ago now confront a new world of apps and mobile devices. What remain constant are the skills you acquire and the methods you learn to approach problems. Given how quickly industries and professions are evolving these days, you will need to apply these skills to new challenges all the time. Learning and re-learning, tooling and retooling are at the heart of the modern economy. Drew Faust, president of Harvard University, has pointed out that a liberal education should give people the skills "that will help them get ready for their sixth job, not their first job."

You might also need to experiment with varieties of intelligence, not just one. Howard Gardner, a developmental psychologist and expert on education, has posited that there are at least eight kinds of intelligence: linguistic, logical-mathematical, spatial, musical, bodily-kinesthetic, naturalistic, intrapersonal, and interpersonal. To be properly prepared for today's world, students must experience several methods of learning conducive to these various intelligences. America's loose and open system of higher education allows for this kind of experimentation. This is what prompted Gardner to write, "There is a joke in my trade that one should go to infant school in France, preschool in Italy, primary school in Japan, secondary school in Germany, and college or university in the United States."

Thomas Cech—Nobel Prize–winning chemist and graduate of Grinnell College, a classic liberal arts school—makes a sports analogy to illustrate a similar insight. Just as athletes do exercises unrelated to their own sport, so students should study fields outside their academic area of focus. "Cross-training may exercise key muscle groups more effectively than spending the same amount of time working out in the sport of interest," Cech writes. "Analogously, a liberal arts education encourages scientists to improve their 'competitive edge' by cross-training in the humanities or arts. Such academic cross-training develops a student's ability to collect and organize facts and opinions, to analyze them and weigh their value, and to articulate an argument, and it may develop these skills more effectively than writing yet another lab report."

Gardner argues that in the future, students will focus even more on modes of thinking. After all, with facts being just a Google search away, why waste brain cells memorizing them? He notes that the best thinking often happens when ideas, fields, and disciplines collide, in a setting where cultures rub up against one another. In the same vein, he rejects a great-books approach to learning—more so than I would. The point of education, in his view, is not to stock students' minds with antique furniture, but to help them gain the intellectual skills they require to build their own set of chairs and tables. He would favor a curriculum that exposes students to different ways of thinking—observational, analytic, aesthetic, teamwork oriented, and so on (which sounds a lot like the Yale-NUS program). Such a curriculum is now known to produce results. Drawing on his knowledge of psychology and neuroscience, Gardner asserts that "it borders on malpractice to design education that is backward-looking and that ignores what we now understand about how the mind constructs and reconstructs knowledge."

Technology and engineering involve extraordinary explorations of ideas and thought, something that is often lost because of their real-world application. They are scientifically fascinating, whether or not they will make you rich. I remember being amazed by the first computers I saw in India in the 1970s, but I didn't have any sense that they would produce lucrative new industries. In those days, the computer programming I learned involved using punch cards and mastering FORTRAN, a language long-since dead. Even in that cumbersome format, the machine's incredible power was evident. It was also fun to learn something so new. Computers have transformed the world in ways that are now blindingly obvious. But with all the money surrounding them, we can easily forget the intellectual pleasure they can give. Big data, artificial intelligence, and mobile computing all might produce great new companies, but they also take us into areas of knowledge where we have never been before. And whether or not that makes someone a billionaire, it is a thrilling intellectual journey that asks profound questions about the nature of the mind—a return in some ways to the idea of science as a branch of philosophy.

Even technical skills by themselves are a wonderful manifestation of human ingenuity. But they don't have to be praised at the expense of humanities, as they often are today. Engineering is not better than art history. Society needs both, often in combination. When unveiling a new edition of the iPad, Steve Jobs explained that "it is in Apple's DNA that technology alone is not enough. It's technology married with liberal arts, married with the humanities, that yields us the result that makes our hearts sing."

That marriage is not simply a matter of adding design to technology. Consider the case of Facebook. Mark Zuckerberg was a classic liberal arts student who also happened to be passionately interested in computers. He studied ancient Greek intensively in high school and was a psychology major when he attended college. The crucial insights that made Facebook the giant it is today have as much to do with psychology as they do technology. In interviews and talks, Zuckerberg has often pointed out that before Facebook was created, most people shielded their identities on the Internet. The Internet was a land of anonymity. Facebook's insight was that you could create a culture of real identities, where people would voluntarily expose themselves to their friends, and this would become a transformative platform. Of course, Zuckerberg understands computers deeply and now uses great coders to put his ideas into practice, but his understanding of human psychology was key to his success. In his own words, Facebook is "as much psychology and sociology as it is technology."

Technology and liberal education go hand in hand in business today. Twenty years ago, tech companies might have survived simply as industrial product manufacturers. Now they have to be at the cutting edge of design, marketing, and social networking. Many other companies also direct much of their attention toward these fields, since manufacturing is increasingly commoditized. You can make a sneaker equally well in many parts of the world. But you can't sell it for three hundred dollars unless you have built a story around it. The same is true for cars, clothes, and coffee. The value added is in the brand—how it is imagined, presented, sold, and sustained. Bruce Nussbaum, an expert on innovation, wrote in a 2005 essay in *Businessweek* that the "Knowledge Economy as we know it is being eclipsed by something new—call it the Creativity Economy. . . . What was once central to corporations—price, quality, and much of the left-brain, digitized analytical work associated with knowledge—is fast being shipped off to lower-paid, highly trained Chinese and Indians, as well as Hungarians, Czechs, and Russians. Increasingly, the new core competence is creativity—the right-brain stuff that smart companies are now harnessing to generate top-line growth. . . . It isn't just about math and science anymore. It's about creativity, imagination, and, above all, innovation."

David Autor, the MIT economist who has most carefully studied the impact of technology and globalization on jobs, writes that "human tasks that have proved most amenable to computerization are those that follow explicit, codifiable procedures— such as multiplication—where computers now vastly exceed human labor in speed, quality, accuracy, and cost efficiency. Tasks that have proved most vexing to automate are those that demand flexibility, judgment, and common sense—skills that we understand only tacitly—for example, developing a hypothesis or organizing a closet. In these tasks, computers are often less sophisticated than preschool age children." This doesn't in any way detract from the need for training in technology, but it does suggest that as we work with computers—which is really the future of all work—the most valuable skills will be the ones that are uniquely human, that computers cannot quite figure out—yet.

Autor divides the job market into three slices. A *Fast Company* article nicely summarizes his research. "At the bottom of the market, there's a growing number of service sector jobs that require hands-on interaction in unpredictable environments—driving a bus, cooking food, caring for children or the elderly. These are impossible to outsource or replace with technology," it notes. The middle tier is made up of jobs that are white collar but are also routine. They involve information processing, form filing, fact finding, data entry, and simple data analysis. These are white-collar jobs in insurance, banking, and law, and they are increasingly being done better by machines. "At the top of the market are the jobs that everyone wants. And guess what?" the article says, perhaps more optimistically than Autor himself might, "These are the jobs that graduates of the American educational system are well prepared for. [They] require creativity, problem solving, decision making, persuasive arguing, and management skills." Vinod Khosla, a Silicon Valley venture capitalist, argues that machine learning will replace many human jobs, but even he believes that work involving complex creativity, emotional intelligence, and value judgments will continue to be done by humans.

And then there is the most influential industry in the United States—entertainment, one of the greatest global growth sectors. A 2012 industry report titled *The Sky Is Rising* presented data showing that all business related to entertainment had maintained an upward trajectory, through recessions and recoveries. Between 1995 and 2009, the number of feature films made worldwide more than quadrupled. Between 2008 and 2011, the number of Americans playing video games jumped about two and a half times. Even in book publishing, revenues rose 5.6 percent between the recession years of 2008 and 2010. Music and television as well—everything in the sector is up. This is an industry that employs millions around the world, continues to grow, and enriches economies and cultures. And at its heart are stories, images, words, and songs. Often these artistic elements are further embellished by technology—as in the films *The Lord of the Rings* and *Frozen*. Regardless of how these films are made, it is clear that much of the production of entertainment requires a background and expertise in one of several of the liberal arts.

So there is a value to writing and music and design and art. But what about art history? What is the best response to President Obama and so many others who worry about the purpose of an academic degree in subjects as seemingly obscure as art history and anthropology? To be fair to the president, his emphasis was on the many millions of Americans who are more inclined to obtain some kind of skills-based training than a liberal education. Perhaps those people would be better off learning a specific technical skill rather than enrolling in a preprofessional-sounding major like "business." But for those who do find that their passion is art history or anthropology, and take it seriously, there are real rewards in the outside world. Both those fields often require the intensive study of several languages and cultures, experience working in foreign countries, an eye for aesthetics, and the ability to translate from one medium or culture to another. Most of these skills could be useful in any number of professions in today's globalized age. They force you to look at people and objects from a variety of perspectives. As Howard Gardner's research demonstrates, this kind of exposure trains various kinds of intelligence, making you a more creative and aware person.

Consider the experience of Dr. Irwin Braverman of the Yale Medical School. In 1998, when he was teaching young medical students who were residents at an affiliated hospital, Dr. Braverman discovered that their powers of observation and diagnosis were weak.

His novel solution was to take them to an art gallery. He teamed up with Linda Friedlander, curator of the Yale Center for British Art, to design a visual tutorial for one hundred students. They asked the students to examine paintings, forcing them to unpack the many layers of detail and meaning in a good work of art. Braverman found that students performed demonstrably better at diagnosis after taking the class—so much so that twenty other medical schools have followed his example.

While this may sound like the quixotic idea of one professor, there are data to support the value of rounded or lateral thinking in the workforce. In 2013, the American Association of Colleges and Universities published a survey showing that 74 percent of employers would recommend a good liberal education to students as the best way to prepare for today's global economy. When students graduate, those with engineering degrees start out with higher salaries—as they should, given that they possess a tangible skillset that can be instantly applied within a company. But over time, the wage gap between engineers and other professionals narrows, especially for liberal arts students who go on to get a professional degree. In fact, one recent study found that students from a set of liberal arts colleges were more likely than their peers

at other institutions of higher education to obtain doc-
torates in sciences, presumably because they possess an
acute curiosity and sense of academic adventure. As
I noted, a liberal education might encourage student
interest in scientific subjects for their inherent intellectual value, rather than their value in the marketplace.
And that might have its own payoffs over time in terms
of basic research and scientific advancement.

Norman Augustine (the former Lockheed Martin
CEO) stressed the importance of both scientific skills
and humanistic thought:

> So what does business need from our educational sys-
> tem? One answer is that it needs more employees who
> excel in science and engineering. . . . But that is only the
> beginning; one cannot live by equations alone. The need
> is increasing for workers with greater foreign-language
> skills and an expanded knowledge of economics, history,
> and geography. And who wants a technology-driven
> economy if those who drive it are not grounded in such
> fields as ethics? . . .
>
> Certainly when it comes to life's major decisions,
> would it not be well for the leaders and employees of
> our government and our nation's firms to have knowl-
> edge of the thoughts of the world's great philosophers
> and the provocative dilemmas found in the works of

great authors and playwrights? I believe the answer is a resounding "yes."

Similarly, Edgar Bronfman, former CEO of Seagram Company, has offered students looking to succeed in business one piece of advice:

> Get a liberal arts degree. In my experience, a liberal arts degree is the most important factor in forming individuals into interesting and interested people who can determine their own paths through the future.
>
> For all of the decisions young business leaders will be asked to make based on facts and figures, needs and wants, numbers and speculation, all of those choices will require one common skill: how to evaluate raw information, be it from people or a spreadsheet, and make reasoned and critical decisions.

Yet a sampling of the views of CEOs remains just anecdotal evidence. What does the big picture tell us, in the vast arena of global economic competition? Can liberal education stand up against the instruction in science and technology that has been so finely tuned by Asian nations?

In 2013, the Organisation for Economic Cooperation and Development released the results of the first-ever survey of the skills adults require to work in the modern economy. Three areas were considered: literacy, numeracy, and technology. The United States performed terribly, scoring below the OECD average in literacy and technological proficiency, and third from the bottom in numeracy. The test was designed to assess problem-solving skills, not rote memorization. The technology test, for instance, asked people to sort computer files into folders. Most troubling is that in numeracy and technological proficiency, young Americans, ages sixteen to twenty-four, ranked last.

This is consistent with the intellectual ability (or lack thereof) that Americans demonstrate earlier in their lives. Every three years since 2000, the OECD has administered a standardized test in science, mathematics, and reading to fifteen-year-olds. The most recent edition of the test—called the Programme for International Student Assessment (PISA)—was conducted in 2012, and it found that among the OECD's thirty-four members, the United States ranked twenty-seventh, twentieth, and seventeenth in math, science, and reading, respectively. If rankings across the three subjects are averaged, the United States comes in twenty-first, trailing nations like the Czech Republic, Poland, Slovenia, and Estonia.

But there is a puzzle. The United States has never performed especially well on international tests. In 1964, the First International Mathematics Study was administered to thirteen-year-olds in twelve countries. On average, thirteen-year-olds in the United States posted a significantly lower score than their counterparts in nine of the countries. Only one education system did worse. In the 1970s and 1980s, studies on mathematic and scientific ability continued to find American students lagging their international peers. Though not always at the bottom of the rankings, the United States has rarely risen far above the middle of the pack. The most recent assessment in the series, called the Trends in International Mathematics and Science Study, was conducted in 2011, and American students did much better. Of fifty education systems tested, the United States ranked eleventh and seventh in fourth-grade math and science, respectively. Of forty-two education systems evaluated, the United States ranked ninth and tenth in eighth-grade math and science. These TIMSS tests, however, are less about conceptual problem solving and more about repeating material that has been studied.

Overall, America's test scores are disappointing, particularly given the United States spends more per capita than almost any other country on education. But how then does one explain the country's success over the last five decades? And how does one understand why students in Asian countries that typically top the international test charts don't end up producing the world's most creative scientists, entrepreneurs, inventors, composers, and businesspeople? These high-scoring Asian countries do well economically, of course, but they don't do especially well at innovation—so far.

Many years ago, I had a conversation about all this with Singapore's minister of education at the time, Tharman Shanmugaratnam. Singapore is the right country to look at because it sits among the top-performing nations on international tests. And yet, it is actively seeking to boost innovation and entrepreneurship among the students producing those top scores. "We both have meritocracies," Shanmugaratnam said. "Yours is a talent meritocracy, ours is an exam meritocracy. There are some parts of the intellect that we are not able to test well—like creativity, curiosity, a sense of adventure, ambition. Most of all, America has a culture of learning that challenges conventional wisdom, even if it means challenging authority. These are the areas where Singapore must learn from America."

It's not just Singapore that feels this way, which is why it set up the Yale-NUS liberal arts and sciences college. South Korea, which consistently produces top rankings on international tests, is making a major investment in liberal education. Seoul National University and Yonsei University have expanded their instruction in subjects associated with the liberal arts. Japan has done the same at the University of Tokyo, and in 2004, Waseda University opened a School of International Liberal Studies, though these efforts have yet to bear fruit in any substantial way. India has a long tradition of liberal arts colleges and universities, many dating to the British era and some to the period after independence, like Jawaharlal Nehru University. But none of these institutions are as prestigious as the country's engineering schools. In addition, all are run like the government bureaucracies that they are. Looking to shake up the old system, in recent years, several prominent Indian businessmen have set up new higher-learning institutions oriented toward the liberal arts, such as Azim Premji University and Mahindra United World College. In addition, Ashoka and Nalanda Universities, both of which welcomed their first class of students in 2014, hearken back to India's ancient heritage of philosophy, literature, science, and ethics but in a modern liberal arts and sciences form.

When considering the world's most innovative countries today, in addition to the United States, in Europe one often hears about Sweden, which seems to have all the new technology companies outside Silicon Valley. And then there is Israel, the subject of a fascinating book detailing its high-technology sector, *Start-up Nation* by Dan Senor and Saul Singer. The evidence confirms this anecdotal impression. Israel actually ranks first in the world in venture capital investments as a percentage of GDP. The United States ranks second, and Sweden sixth—ahead of Great Britain and Germany. A 2014 Bloomberg measure of technology density, or the number of high-tech companies as a percentage of all publicly listed companies, provides a similar story. The United States ranks first, Sweden ranks fifth, and Israel tenth. Research and development expenditures as a percentage of GDP move Israel into the top spot, with Sweden in fourth, and the United States in the tenth place.

What is striking about all three countries is that none of them do particularly well in the PISA rankings. Sweden and Israel performed even worse than the United States on the 2012 assessment. With their three subject rankings averaged, they come in twenty-eighth and twenty-ninth, respectively, among the OECD's thirty-four members. What do these countries have in common, other than bad test scores, that could explain their real-world success? A few traits stand out. In all three places, the work culture is non-hierarchical and merit based. All operate like "young" countries, with energy and dynamism. All three are open societies, happy to let in the world's ideas, goods, and services. And finally, they are all places where people are confident—a characteristic that can actually be measured. The PISA tests don't simply evaluate students' skills; they also ask them questions to determine their levels of confidence—or "self-concept," in the jargon used. Students are asked how good they think they are at, say, mathematics. Despite ranking twenty-seventh and thirtieth in the subject, respectively, American and Israeli students come out right at the top in their belief in their own abilities. Sweden comes in seventh, even though its actual math ranking was twenty-eighth.

I remember first reading about this disparity between achievement and confidence in the early 1990s. At the time, William Bennett, who had served as secretary of education under President Ronald Reagan, described similar results, quipping, "This country is a lot better at teaching self-esteem than it is at teaching math." It's a funny line, but on reflection, there is actually something powerful in the plucky confidence of American, Swedish, and Israeli students. It allows them to challenge their elders, start companies, persist when others think they are wrong, and pick themselves up when they fail. Though confidence overstated runs the risk of self-delusion, the trait is an essential ingredient for entrepreneurship. In their book *The Triple Package*, Amy Chua and Jed Rubenfeld argue that the best-performing minority groups possess a strange combination of insecurity and confidence. When we consider America's endless concerns about its decline, or Israel's fear for its existence, and then couple these insecurities with the bravado its people display, perhaps we see the same phenomenon writ large.

The relationship between educational test scores and economic performance is a subject of great controversy (and has been caught up in the debate about education reform). Some experts see no correlation at all, while others point to data suggesting the opposite. My own sense is that all things being equal, it obviously helps to have a well-trained population. America's public school system needs many of the reforms being proposed by both Republicans and Democrats to make this more likely. South Korea, Taiwan, Singapore, and now China—with their high rates of growth in recent decades—are living proof of a connection between strong test scores and economic success. But growth and innovation are supported by many factors, some of which are wholly outside the realm of tests and skills.

The United States has a poorly trained labor force in

general, which is a disadvantage. But it makes up for it in several ways. The country has an extremely dynamic and flexible economy, strong rule of law, a good regulatory structure, extraordinary research universities, rich venture-capital firms, and a vibrant entrepreneurial culture. All these ingredients more than make up for middling test scores. Japan, on the other hand, has a superbly trained general population. But it would score poorly on many broader economic and cultural indicators, especially with regard to entrepreneurship and the hierarchy of society. Good test scores are not enough to create the next Google.

America also benefits by being the world's magnet for the very best and brightest. It takes in many immigrants, some of whom are well educated and motivated. Its best performers create new companies, products, and even industries. As Silicon Valley demonstrates, a small number of people can have a big impact on the economy. Scholars Heiner Rindermann and James Thompson have found that the performance of a country's top 5 percent, as measured by IQ, is closely correlated with economic growth. America's top 1 percent intellectually, which works out to over three million people, has an outsized effect on growth, according to Jonathan Wai of Duke University.

In a sense, the United States does an amazing job

given its raw material (a poorly trained labor force), and Japan underperforms despite its amazing raw material (a highly skilled pool of workers). South Korea and Singapore, as well as Switzerland and some northern European countries, do well in both dimensions and have the growth to prove it. The great advantage of their model is that it not only generates strong economic growth for the country but also benefits the median worker. In other words, America has many Bill Gateses and Warren Buffetts and Googles and Facebooks to bring up its averages. But top performers and a handful of technology behemoths do not translate into rising incomes for most Americans. For that, the East Asian–northern European model of good education *for all* is crucial. The French economist Thomas Piketty is famous for arguing that capitalism in its essence produces inequality and for advocating higher taxes to ameliorate the problem. But in his treatise *Capital in the Twenty-First Century*, Piketty acknowledges that the best approach to reducing inequality in the long run is widening access to good education. "Over a long period of time," he writes, "the main force in favor of greater equality has been the diffusion of knowledge and skills."

East Asia's economic success has led many to want to emulate its educational system. But as with Amer-

ica, Asian growth might be explained more fundamentally by other factors—like hard work. Again,
results from PISA 2012 serve as evidence. On average, students in Shanghai performed better than all
their international peers, and were found to be two
years ahead of even the best-performing entry from
the United States, Massachusetts. What is the secret
formula that explains Shanghai's superior performance? Does it teach new math? Old math? Chinese
math? The answer might be simpler. U.S. Secretary
of Education Arne Duncan has estimated that Chinese students spend 25 to 30 percent longer a year in
school than their American counterparts. By the age
of fifteen, when the test is taken, students have been
at school for about ten years. So, with the number
of school days in the United States set at 180 each
year, a fifteen-year-old student in Shanghai will have
attended school for what amounts to roughly two to
three more academic years than a fifteen-year-old
in Massachusetts. They're two years ahead in math
because they've taken at least two more years of
math! It's not Chinese genes, not a better system, not
a magic formula—just more work. If Malcolm Gladwell is right when he says that spending ten thousand
hours in practice helps you gain proficiency in an
area, East Asians are going to reach that goal much

faster than Americans, no matter what the mode of instruction is.

Americans should be careful before they try to mimic Asian educational systems, which are still oriented around memorization and test taking. I went through that kind of system and it's not conducive to thinking, problem solving, or creativity. The founder of China's Internet behemoth Alibaba, Jack Ma, gave a speech recently in which he asked why the Chinese were not as innovative as Americans and Europeans. His answer was that the Chinese educational system teaches the basics very well, but it does not nourish a person's complete intelligence and creativity. It needs to allow people to range freely, experiment, and enjoy themselves while learning. "[Innovations] will only come regularly if we rethink our culture . . . and our sports," he said. "Many painters learn by having fun, many works [of art and literature] are the products of having fun. So, our entrepreneurs need to learn to have fun, too."

The Asian system does teach you to work hard, to retain knowledge for tests, and to perform under pressure—all of which are valuable skills. That may be the simple problem in the United States today—people are working less at school. (This is true of the country in general, not of its best-performing high schools. That said, even among the latter, the academic year is much shorter than almost anywhere else in the world.) And American universities today have become less demanding along many dimensions. Grade inflation is just one metric. A 2010 research paper found that the average number of hours college students spend studying outside the classroom a week declined from forty in 1961 to twenty-seven in 2003.

An important new study drew on survey data, transcripts, and a learning assessment to answer the question of what high-quality American colleges teach their students. The answer is stunning: not very much. Richard Arum and Josipa Roksa, the authors of *Academically Adrift*, summarize their findings succinctly:

> Large numbers of four-year college students experience only limited academic demands, invest only modest levels of effort, and demonstrate limited or no growth on an objective measure of critical thinking, complex reasoning, and written communication. Fifty percent of sophomores in our sample reported that they had not taken a single course the prior semester that required more than twenty pages of writing over the course of the semester; one-third did not take a single course the prior semester that required on average even more than 40 pages of reading per week. Students in our sample reported studying on average only 12 hours per week during their

sophomore year, one third of which was spent studying with peers. Even more alarming, 37 percent dedicated five or fewer hours per week to studying alone. These patterns persisted through the senior year and are broadly consistent with findings on academic engagement from other studies. These findings also should be considered in the context of empirical evidence documenting large declines over recent decades in the number of hours full-time college students spend studying.

And then there is the industry of "amateur" sports, which consumes a massive amount of time, money, and attention. Many large universities have become multi-million-dollar sports franchises with small educational institutions attached to them. Some of these sports, football most clearly, have the effect of systematically damaging the brains of the students. Yet as Malcolm Gladwell has pointed out, institutions that are supposedly dedicated to enhancing the cerebral capacity of their students continue to promote, celebrate, and profit from these activities. The idea of merit and the discipline of academic work are undermined as a result.

In many colleges, the subjects that often define the liberal arts—the core humanities—have in particular become less structured and demanding. That might be why employers have become more suspicious of majors like English and history. The social sciences, by contrast, have increased in popularity among students and in credibility with employers. They remain somewhat rigorous, representing a midpoint of sorts between the humanities and the sciences. It is the rigor and discipline of a science degree that might impress employers the most, not the specific subject matter. Employers know that a physics major is not likely to use much quantum mechanics in a job involving trading commodities. My brother graduated summa cum laude from college with a degree in math and then went into high finance on Wall Street—supposedly a field in which numbers matter. He felt that his undergraduate major gave him no technical advantage over a humanities major who could do basic arithmetic.

An excessively loose structure, diminishing work levels, and low standards—these are flaws in the implementation of a liberal education, not characteristics of it. The solution is not that people need to major in marketing in college, but that their liberal education should be more structured and demanding. Majors should have some required sequence of basic courses, as in economics. That would be the best preparation for better jobs and stronger careers. Many firms look favorably on college athletes because they know that athletes have the discipline and habits that go along with regular, long training and practice sessions. If you want to succeed in life, most often you need to put in the hours, develop good habits, work well with others, and get lucky. That is true whether you study English, physics, history, engineering, or business.

In the late 1980s, at the peak of the belief—or fear—that Japan was going to become the world's largest economy, its most innovative country, and the most dynamic society, the journalist James Fallows spent several years there to examine how the United States might confront competition from the "rising sun." He came to the conclusion that the best strategy was not to try to become like the Japanese—that is, not to create a society grounded in self-sacrifice, all-powerful government mandarins, and massive industrial policy. The answer was, as the title of his book indicates, to be *More Like Us*. That meant emphasizing the distinctive strengths of the United States—its openness, innovation, decentralization, laissez-faire attitude, and entrepreneurial culture—but to do so even better than in the past. The same might be true in this case. The solution to the problems of a liberal education is more—and better—liberal education.

4

The Natural Aristocracy

BENJAMIN FRANKLIN IS the most important American statesman never to have been president. Franklin played a pivotal role in the revolution, helping to draft the Declaration of Independence and then serving as a delegate to the Constitutional Convention. He was minister to France during the Revolutionary War, securing what proved to be critical French loans in support of the effort. But Franklin looms large in American history more for symbolism than for statecraft. He represents an American archetype, perhaps *the* American archetype—the self-made man. One of ten children, Franklin received only two years of formal education, which ended when he was ten years old. Seven years later, he left his home in Boston for Philadelphia to make his own way in the world. Civically engaged, business oriented, technology obsessed, and socially skilled, Franklin was "our founding Yuppie," declares the *New York Times* columnist David Brooks. Franklin "would have felt right at home in the information revolution," Walter Isaacson writes in his biography of the statesman. "We can easily imagine having a beer with him after work, showing him how to use the latest digital device, sharing the business plan for a new venture, and discussing the most recent political scandals or policy ideas." The essence of Franklin's appeal is that he was brilliant but practical, interested in everything, but especially in how things work.

This might make Ben Franklin sound like the perfect proponent of the "drop out of school and start a company" view of life. To the extent that any schooling helped him, it was the training he received during his apprenticeship as a printer. But it turns out that Franklin had a surprisingly broad view of the kind of education individuals need in order to flourish. In 1749, he published a pamphlet, *Proposals Relating to the Education of Youth in Pennsylvania*, in which he outlined his plans for a new academy in the colony.*

---

* All spellings and capitalization in writings by the founding fathers have been modernized where necessary.

Franklin believed that education should help people navigate the real world as they entered careers in
politics, law, business, and other fields. At the same
time, he wanted young men to gain exposure to "the
great outlines of knowledge."* The purpose of their
education would be to produce "true merit," which
meant joining ability with the inclination to serve
"Mankind, one's Country, Friends and Family."

Franklin wanted students to be part of a residential college, even specifying that it would ideally be
somewhere with a garden, an orchard, a meadow, and
a "field or two." They should live together "frugally,"
he wrote, and exercise frequently to "render active their
bodies." The subjects Franklin suggested they study
were broad and diverse: arithmetic, astronomy, geography, religion, agriculture, and history along many
dimensions (of laws, customs, nature, and morality). In
particular, he stressed the importance of the study of
English over Latin and Greek. He urged that greater
attention be placed on writing than on oratory, as he
believed communication in the modern world was
more effective through the written than the spoken
word. One wonders what he would have urged once he
saw the impact of television and the Internet.

---

* At the time, advocates of education, Benjamin Franklin and Thomas
Jefferson included, thought it fitting only for young white men.

The school Franklin envisioned in the middle of
the eighteenth century largely resembles what we
understand a liberal arts college to be today. Franklin struggled to put his ideas into practice at the time.
His pamphlet got the wheels turning for plans on a
school in Philadelphia, but when the academy offi-
cially opened in 1751, an old guard of pious educators blocked his efforts at reform. The trustees he had
helped recruit continued to prioritize the study of Latin
over English. But in subsequent decades, the academy
grew into the University of Pennsylvania, which went
on to become one of the world's most distinguished
liberal arts schools.

Franklin likely wanted others to obtain a more general education than he himself had received, because
he realized his own success was a result of an intense
and broad-ranging curiosity. He was fascinated by
everything he saw around him, from dolphins to
lunar eclipses, and he experimented with ideas from
electricity to refrigeration. At twenty-one, Franklin
founded a small club of young professionals called the
Junto, which met regularly to discuss topics including
politics, science, and business—almost like a college
seminar. And while he was always trying to make
stuff, Franklin was also philosophizing and imagin-
ing in the abstract. This is how, despite his lack of

formal education, he became a major scientific figure of his time, recognized with honorary degrees from Oxford, Yale, and Harvard and awarded the Copley Medal (an earlier version of the Nobel Prize in science). Isaacson quotes Dudley Herschbach, Harvard's Nobel Prize–winning scientist, on Franklin's scientific accomplishments: "His work on electricity was recognized as ushering in a scientific revolution comparable to those wrought by Newton in the previous century or by Watson and Crick in ours."

If Franklin saw education as the path to service for mankind, his great contemporary Thomas Jefferson made a more urgent connection: a liberal education would ensure the survival of democracy. In 1778, Jefferson presented to the Virginia legislature "A Bill for the More General Diffusion of Knowledge," in which he argued that all forms of government could degenerate into tyranny. The best way of preventing this, he wrote, is "to illuminate, as far as practicable, the minds of the people at large." The study of history could serve as an especially effective bulwark, allowing the people to learn how to defeat tyranny from past examples. Jefferson would return again and again to the importance of education in a democracy. In his elegant and erudite book, *Beyond the University*, Michael Roth, president of Wesleyan

University, explains, "This would create a virtuous
circle of learning and a citizenry thoughtful enough to
protect itself from governmental overreaching." Over
the course of his political career, Jefferson advocated a
number of measures to spread education far and wide,
including publicly funded schools and the establishment of a national university in Washington. After
serving as secretary of state and president, he returned
to this central obsession by founding the University of
Virginia.

In 1818, at the age of seventy-five, Jefferson gath-
ered together friends and associates to establish a new
school in Charlottesville, Virginia. It was a university
"so thoroughly the work of his hands that it was to
become known simply as Mr. Jefferson's," Jon Meacham writes in his biography of the third president. Its
objectives were a mix of the practical and philosophical: to train statesmen and professionals, to expound
on the principles of freedom, to teach methods of agriculture, and to enlarge the minds and morals of the
young. His proposed curriculum was more academic
than Franklin's, with a good deal of math and science,
as well as modern and ancient languages, law and history, writing and grammar. Jefferson was one of the
earliest proponents of electives, believing that students
should practice the same freedom at school that they

were allowed in a democracy. And as with Franklin's school, Jefferson's university was nonsectarian.
In fact, the University of Virginia was unique in that
its physical layout was centered not on the chapel but
on the library.

Franklin and Jefferson shared the view that education was a way to ensure that the new republic
would be a place of merit, where birth, bloodlines,
and hereditary privilege would not count for much.
Franklin was a self-made man, and throughout his
life he extolled the virtues of those who had risen
through hard work, talent, and skill. He thoroughly
enjoyed the company of tradesmen, small entrepreneurs, and shopkeepers, seeing in their rise the idea
of equality that was at the heart of the idea of America. Jefferson's prose differed. He often wrote about
the need to create a "natural aristocracy." While this
sounds like a plan for a House of Lords, Jefferson in
fact intended the opposite. His "natural aristocracy"
was based strictly on merit, to be refreshed constantly,
as opposed to an "unnatural aristocracy," based on
birth, wealth, and privilege. Jefferson believed that
all societies inevitably have elites—someone, in
other words, has to be on top—but that America's
elite should come from finding the best and brightest and educating them well. "The best geniuses will

be raked from the rubbish annually," he wrote. The United States would be able to benefit from "those talents which nature had sown as liberally among the poor as the rich, but which perish without use, if not sought for and cultivated."

For Jefferson, there was one step crucial to creating a genuine natural aristocracy. The poor and rich had to have equal access to a good education. That's why, despite being something of a libertarian, he repeatedly proposed that the state pay for universal primary education as well as fund education at later stages. He was met with opposition from many quarters, mostly those wary of big government or higher taxes. Yet interestingly, one of his most ardent supporters was an old friend and political opponent, the conservative John Adams. "The whole people must take upon themselves the education of the whole people, and must be willing to bear the expenses of it," Adams wrote. "There should not be a district of one mile square, without a school in it, not founded by a charitable individual, but maintained at the public expense of the people themselves." Jefferson's fear was that without such a system of public education, the country would end up being ruled by a privileged elite that would recycle itself through a network of private institutions that entrenched their advantages.

What would these founding fathers make of America today? What would they make of a country where, as Thomas Edsall noted in the *New York Times*, 74 percent of students attending the most competitive colleges were raised in families in the top income quartile and only 3 percent come from families in the bottom quartile? Even among the best students, family background makes a huge difference: High-scoring students from families in the top income quartile are almost twice as likely to get college degrees as students with similar high scores from families in the bottom quartile. In addition, criteria for admission into the best colleges and universities that seem purely merit based—like grades, SAT scores, and participation in extracurricular activities—are actually correlated with family income. (The correlation is not as strong for test scores as for outside activities. You are only able to take that fascinating unpaid summer internship in South Africa if you have the means.) Edsall quotes the education expert Anthony Carnevale: "The education system is an increasingly powerful mechanism for the intergenerational reproduction of privilege."

Half a century ago, the American middle class had a powerful path to a high-quality education. In the decades following the Second World War, the GI Bill gave a whole new group of Americans access to the best colleges, and tuition was affordable even for the middle class. Most importantly, public universities were booming. In 1960, an eighteen-year-old living in California could get a superb education at any of the University of California campuses—including the one in Berkeley, which has many departments that rank in the top five worldwide—at no cost whatever. Zero. (In fact, in those days a California resident could go through one of the world's best public schools before attending Berkeley for college and later for graduate school, and his or her entire world-class education—from kindergarten to a PhD—would have cost him or her virtually nothing.) As late as the 1970s, Berkeley's annual tuition for undergraduates who were California residents was around $700. For the 2014–15 academic year, tuition (not including room and board) costs California residents $12,972. Nonresidents are charged an additional $22,878. Berkeley's own estimate of the total cost of attendance for a nonresident student living on campus is over $55,000 a year. And unlike the very top private schools, Berkeley does not have the endowment to provide need-blind financial aid. As a result, the makeup of its student body today is probably quite different from what it was three or four decades ago.

Most state universities face even deeper pressures than Berkeley, which occupies a special place in the public eye and can raise private funds as well. Once highways to the middle class, these schools are reeling from decades of reduced support from their state governments as well as rising costs. As a result, many have created the "party pathway," described in Elizabeth Armstrong and Laura Hamilton's book *Paying for the Party*, in which an increasing number of rich out-of-state kids who can pay full tuition get relaxed admissions criteria, special majors, inflated grades, and fancy facilities. The bright low-income students, who are on the "mobility pathway," get none of this. Facing academic, economic, and social pressures, they have a higher burnout and dropout rate. Those who graduate do so with a mountain of debt.

The best colleges in the United States aspire to an idea of merit, of creating Jefferson's natural aristocracy. And they do give scholarships to many students who could not otherwise afford to be there, though this still helps a very small number of poor students. In addition, the number of people applying to the top schools has exploded, and the admissions rates are now so low, often under 10 percent, that the admissions process can seem quite arbitrary. Compounding the problem is the fact that elite schools provide many special preferences for legacies, underrepresented minorities, and—in the most significant deviation from merit—

recruited athletes. A former senior admissions officer at an Ivy League school told me, "I have to turn down hundreds of highly qualified applicants, including many truly talented amateur athletes, because we must take so many recruited athletes who are narrowly focused and less accomplished otherwise." The problem, as he notes, is not athletics per se, which combines talent and discipline in an exemplary way. It is that the process of recruitment has become so intense that the system is now distorted. William Bowen, a former president of Princeton University, has documented and argued persuasively that over the last few decades, college sports programs that recruit athletes have warped those colleges' academic values. An admissions official told me that many now take in athletes who score 150 to 200 points lower on the SATs than other students—a much more significant drop in standards than for legacies or minorities—to build their sports teams. The recruited athletes often struggle to keep up with the academic demands in the classroom, while good amateur athletes are frozen out of college sports. The entire process shifts the focus of the campus away from academics. And yet, no president of a liberal arts college dares suggest this system be changed.

In a 2012 essay in the *American Conservative*, California political activist Ron Unz presented statistics seeming to show that the nation's top colleges and universities have over the past two decades maintained a de facto quota for Asian American students, limiting them to about 16.5 percent of the study body, despite their exploding applicant numbers and high achievements. The numbers may not be exactly right. Two Ivy League admissions officers estimated to me that Asian Americans actually make up more than 20 percent of their entering classes—many don't declare their race or are racially mixed. But in comparison, at schools that are less reliant on nebulous admissions criteria such as "character" and being "well-rounded," like Caltech and Berkeley, Asian Americans make up about 40 percent of the study body. Winners of the United States Olympiads in mathematics, computing, physics, biology, and chemistry and of the Intel Science Talent Search have been more than 60 percent Asian American in recent years.

A school full of Olympiad winners would in fact lack balance, and achievements based entirely on numbers and tests are not the only measures of a student's potential. Yet it's worth bearing in mind that, historically, colleges have employed intangible criteria in admissions specifically to keep out bright and ambitious newcomers. In his book *The Chosen: The Hidden History of Admission and Exclusion at Harvard,*

Yale, and Princeton, Jerome Karabel demonstrates in painstaking detail how subjective admissions requirements like interviews and involvement in extracurricular activities were put in place by Ivy League schools largely to keep Jewish admissions from rising in the 1920s through the 1940s. Unless there are aggressive efforts to compensate for the advantages of wealth, including attendance at private schools and participation in luxury extracurricular pursuits, the American elite educational system runs the risk, in Jefferson's terms, of creating an unnatural aristocracy.

At one level, these concerns and complaints might seem irrelevant. American colleges and universities are booming. Their success and fame have attracted applicants from around the world. A good college degree has become more crucial in everyone's mind. The post-industrial economy rewards people who have academic training and credentials, or "knowledge workers," even more so than before. College sports have become more popular and more profitable for the schools. But they face one trend that seems utterly unsustainable: the rising cost of college. The average college tuition has increased at an eye-popping pace—over 1,200 percent since 1978, the first year complete records were kept. That is four times the pace of the consumer price index and twice as fast as medical costs. This extraordinary cost spiral, in an age when the prices of almost all goods and services have declined, is surely one of the most striking phenomena in modern American life, and it has largely been accepted without much controversy.

That rise in cost is at the heart of many of the concerns about the value of a liberal education. After all, when one is questioning whether a product is "worth it"—be it an outfit, a car, or an education—crucial to that determination is its price. A liberal education was affordable to a middle-class family in 1965. It is much less so today. That means families have to make trade-offs between spending money on an education and earmarking it for other things. It's often noted that the data show that a college degree improves one's lifetime earnings, so that even a large investment in a college education is worth it. That may be true, but it also explains why families so anxious about this onerous price tag worry endlessly that their son or daughter could jeopardize everything by majoring in the "wrong" subject or getting a less marketable degree. The fact that we now use the language of "return on investment" to describe the experience of getting educated is revealing.

Why has the cost of college risen so quickly? One plausible explanation, offered by the economists

William Baumol and William Bowen, is that certain labor-intensive industries such as education can't replace humans with machines or expand production lines in the way other industries can. The economist Robert Frank gives an excellent example to explain this basic idea: "while productivity gains have made it possible to assemble cars with only a tiny fraction of the labor that was once required, it still takes four musicians nine minutes to perform Beethoven's String Quartet No. 4 in C minor, just as it did in the 19th century." A seminar class at a good college will tend to have a ratio of one professor to, say, fifteen students. If you believe that's the best way to teach, it can't be made more efficient. This is why costs in education rise much faster than in the general economy, where automation and outsourcing can replace expensive labor in some way or the other. It's true in other sectors of the economy as well. If you are happy listening to a recording of the same Mozart quartet, you can do it virtually for free. But the live experience has become much more expensive over the years. Whether it's the Berlin Philharmonic or Beyoncé, the money is in the actual concert, not the digital recording.

There are probably other factors as well. Bowen points out that it's difficult to measure productivity in a field like education—that universities might have inefficient administrative systems, or they might be price insensitive when it comes to academic quality, spending whatever it takes to be the best. All of this is true. But it might also be that the entire system of education in the United States is a poorly designed mishmash, combining some of the worst elements of the market and the state. It shares this character with health care. In both cases, the consumer wants the product and yet can't really judge its quality. (Can you really decide that you don't need an MRI? Or a college degree?) Additionally, the consumer doesn't pay directly for the product, at least not the full price. Third-party payments, often from the government, have complicated processes and timelines, which further obscure price signals and market discipline. Finally, it's not clear how to judge the value of an education. Is it just the college degree that matters? Or is there some broader measure of a good education? And how would you measure the latter? Perhaps for these reasons, over the last thirty years, while inflation has been wrung out of the American economy in almost every other sector, education and health care costs have risen annually at many times the rate of inflation.

Measuring the quality of education turns out to be extremely complicated. Most colleges are judged by a variety of factors, including resources, faculty, and facilities. Chief among them, though, is the average SAT score of entering freshmen. Yet the test scores used in admissions are a measure of what colleges take in, not what they produce. The fact that an Ivy League school has freshmen with high SAT scores tells us that it is a good magnet for talent but nothing else. What should matter is how students, including those with low SAT scores, improve over the course of their time in school. But what is the measure by which to judge that improvement? *Academically Adrift*, the book mentioned in the last chapter, has brought this issue to the national fore. Using the Collegiate Learning Assessment test, the book's authors found that 45 percent of students showed no improvement in critical thinking in their first two years of college. Subsequent tests have demonstrated that this pattern continues in their junior and senior years as well. Why? As the book shows, in many colleges, students take easy courses with few assignments and little homework or reading. This results in little improved output.

If these are the problems of a liberal education today, there might be a solution in the form of technology. Education is a sphere of life remarkably unchanged over the course of centuries. We learn today in ways that would seem largely familiar to the ancient Greeks. A teacher stands in front of a group of students and lectures them, at times involving them in discussion. All the revolutions in information technology in recent decades have had hardly any effect on this basic mechanism, or on the fundamental operations of schools, colleges, and universities.

Until now. Enter MOOCs, or Massive Open Online Courses, among other online systems of instruction that promise, or threaten, to change the way education is provided in the United States and around the world. MOOCs are courses that can be taken online by watching videos of lectures and completing assignments and tests that are graded by computer programs or humans. In some cases, students engage in virtual classroom discussions through structured chat rooms or bulletin boards. So far, MOOCs rarely offer any official form of credit—though that is likely to change over time. The larger idea behind them is simple. A course that could be taken by a few hundred people at a university is now available to tens of thousands, even hundreds of thousands, across the globe. By early 2014, the two main platforms for MOOCs in the United States had around ten million students collectively. Coursera, the largest platform, had students from nearly two hundred countries taking almost six hundred courses in a vast diversity of fields. MOOCs represent the most ambitious effort to widen access to education in history. And they have a lot of people at universities very worried.

In October 2012, I was asked to moderate a panel for a conference on education sponsored by *Time* magazine and the Carnegie Endowment. My panel included four distinguished college presidents and Andrew Ng, one of the founders of Coursera. At the time, Coursera was just half a year old. Professor Ng, a Stanford computer scientist, made a presentation in which he spoke of the great potential of MOOCs and of his ambition to provide new educational opportunities to millions of people. Using his own course as an example, Ng explained how online technology had massively expanded the number of students who could enroll in a single class, from five hundred or so at Stanford to tens of thousands online. He was modest and stressed that this new model of education is in its early stages and would need many adjustments.

The educational establishment could not have been more skeptical. All the college presidents on the panel expressed concerns and doubts about this new technology, assuring the audience (mainly, other college presidents) that a physical campus, in-class teaching, and the peer experience would always be essential and irreplaceable aspects of higher education. "Lots of people sign up but most drop out," the former president of one prestigious university complained. Ng acknowledged that the completion rate was low, but he noted that the completion rates for his Stanford courses are also low. Hundreds of people attend the first class or two but never return. Another attendee insisted that video lectures by star professors could never replace the personal interaction between scholars and students. Ng agreed, reminding everyone that MOOCs are intended primarily for people in developing countries who would otherwise have little access to the college seminar. He also noted, however, that there is little contact between professors and students in large lecture courses at American universities. In general, the panelists and audience treated Ng with courtesy but persistent skepticism. I couldn't tell if they were sure his new-fangled ideas wouldn't work or if they were worried that they would. A 2013 survey bears out this anecdotal impression. Only one in five professors polled by Gallup believe that online classes could be as effective as the in-class experience.

For me, the discussion had the feeling of déjà vu. I had spent ten years at *Newsweek*, one of the world's most successful print publications, with tens of millions of readers and hundreds of millions of dollars in revenues. While the Internet was blossoming, we had told ourselves that we still had unique advantages, that people wanted qualities particular to our product, that the magazine business had gone through cyclical challenges before, and that we would weather the storm. As it happened, the *Time* conference was held on the day that the final edition of *Newsweek* was published. (It has since been resuscitated with a more limited circulation.) My only suggestion to the audience about online education was that they keep in mind *Newsweek*'s fate. The Internet was transforming all industries in some way or another. The chance that it would leave education alone was highly unlikely—and to fail to recognize that was not the way to plan for the future.

The educators' concerns were understandable. Two recent studies found that of millions who signed up for MOOCs on the two largest online platforms, only 4 percent (for Coursera) and 5 percent (for edX) fully finished the courses. The media used these low completion rates to cast doubt on the promise of the technology and to suggest that MOOCs had been overrated after all. But this is a misreading of the results. Recall that anyone anywhere in the world, with any level of education, can sign up for a MOOC. There is no barrier to entry. So it should come as no surprise that many of the people who do sign up are not serious about it. Coursera reports that the dropout rate after the first week is very high, almost 40 percent. But then, of those students who stay with the course after the first week, nearly 50 percent complete it. And keep in mind that the initial enrollment numbers are so large that even a 5 percent completion rate is gigantic. In 2012 and 2013, approximately 43,000 students finished the first seventeen courses offered by edX—an average of 2,529 students per class, which would be a fivefold expansion of even a large lecture course. Yale's Nobel Prize–winning economist Robert Shiller taught his course online in 2013 for the first time. More people took (and completed) it in that one year than the total number of students he had taught in his thirty-two years as a professor.

The potential of online education is dazzling. Anyone, no matter how rich or poor, young or old, Haitian or Mongolian, can access the world's best courses, watch the greatest lectures, and study those subjects he or she had always dreamed about. Khan Academy, the extraordinary online platform with three thousand different videos that teach everything from algebra to biology to history, has already changed the way we think about learning. One crucial new method is that of "flipping the classroom," so that students listen (or watch) a lecture at home and then work on problems with teachers in school. It is a much more efficient and effective use of both a teacher's and a student's time and energy—passive learning at home by yourself, active learning at school with a teacher helping. Like any great technological shift, MOOCs and similar ventures will have ripple effects across the field of education. They will force teachers to do better, since they will now be measured against the world's best. They will pressure colleges to contain costs, perhaps focus on the things they do well, and find new ways to enhance productivity. They will make students decide what really matters to them— knowledge, credentials, classroom discussions—and find the best ways to get it. The best colleges will face fewer challenges, partly because they offer a unique experience and largely because they are selling membership to a valuable private networking experience. But new models of education will rise, like the Minerva Project, a for-profit liberal arts school that provides a pared-down college experience using online classes and eliminating costly accessories like facilities and sports teams. And this is just the beginning. Online learning technology will prompt changes in ways we have not even anticipated yet. MOOCs are barely three years old.

Key to the innovations in teaching that could come from MOOCs is the promise of "big data." As millions of people take online courses, the institutions that offer them will have immense amounts of information in their systems. Properly analyzed, this information could produce a revolution in learning. Education has always sought to cater to the individual. I learn differently than you do, and ideally, we would all be taught in ways that are targeted to each of us specifically. That's why, for most of human history, the very rich had their children taught by private tutors. In his book *The One World Schoolhouse*, Khan Academy founder Salman Khan points out that education today relies on a model for the classroom from the industrial era. In the mid-nineteenth century, when Prussia decided to provide education for the masses, it modeled its schools on the factories of the time. Students were bunched together by age and put on a virtual conveyer belt. Instruction was thrown at them, and they picked up whatever they could as they were pushed forward to graduation. Other countries used similar methods. Perhaps this was the only way to educate large numbers of people, but education was not customized to the individual in any sense. In fact, the more people who had to be educated, the less customized the experience.

Now that can change. With big data—and strong analysis and smart programs processing that data—educators can learn a great deal about what is and what isn't working. As students progress through a course, their teachers could get feedback related to each individual's performance. The system could use early indicators like answers on quizzes and problem sets to create specific remedial content, change the pace, and tailor reading and exams in ways that would be most effective for that particular student. If thousands of students around the world stumbled over certain questions in quizzes, it would send a broader signal to educators that the teaching of that section or the design of the tests required fixing. Big data could be an early detection system that allowed for quick course corrections.

A well-structured online course that used the benefits of big data would thus develop like a tree, with each student proceeding down a particular set of branches, specifically tailored to his or her strengths and weaknesses. This is a revolutionary concept because it alters one of the fundamental rules of education. Until now, it had always been assumed that increasing the number of students could be done only at the cost of providing less personal attention to each individual. In industry jargon, scale and customization were inversely correlated. But now, scale and customization can be positively correlated. The more students who take a course, the larger the database created, which can then be analyzed and applied to personalize each student's experience. This might be the path to highly effective individual learning on a mass scale.

Yet the greatest promise of MOOCs, and online learning in general, remains the original intent: expanding access. Stamenka Uvalić-Trumbić, an education expert formerly with UNESCO, noted in 2011 that the number of people enrolled in higher education across the world was 165 million. At current growth rates, that number would reach 263 million in 2025. But it will be impossible to get to those numbers using the present system of education. "Accommodating the additional 98 million students would require more than four major universities (30,000 students) to open every week for the next fifteen years," Uvalić-Trumbić explained. That pace of expansion is not happening anywhere. Even in China, where the government has made a major commitment to enlarging access to higher education, the number of students is growing at a much faster rate than the number of faculty and facilities. "Inevitably, the greatest impact of MOOCs will be in the developing world, where it will be possible for millions to get educated who simply would not have otherwise," says Richard Levin, the CEO of Coursera. Already, 72 percent of registered users of edX courses come from outside the United States.

The makeup of those enrolled in MOOCs is quite diverse. The vast majority are not in the college-age cohort. They range in levels of education, though most have acquired some post-secondary degree. The courses offered cover a mix of preprofessional and general education topics. A study published in November 2013 found that of the students enrolled in at least one of the thirty-two MOOCs offered by the University of Pennsylvania through Coursera, 50 percent said they were taking it out of general curiosity or "just for fun." Forty-four percent said they were enrolled to "gain specific skills to do my job better." In other words, a large portion of MOOC users are interested in acquiring a liberal education—or enhancing the one they received years ago. We are moving toward a time when anyone can get elements of a liberal education and yet be disconnected from the experience—and cost—of attending a liberal arts college. I said "elements" of a liberal education, as it might well be that residential colleges, classroom seminars, late-night discussions, and extracurricular activities are collectively essential to providing the complete experience. Certainly for the best colleges—say, the top fifty in America or the top one hundred worldwide—the benefits of being admitted to a small club will justify a steep price. But that doesn't mean important aspects of this education cannot be provided to millions of people around the world at a fraction of the cost. And if the value of a liberal education is real—in opening the mind, preparing people for the fast-changing world, and building a capacity for freedom—then the fact that millions of people in China and India and Russia and Brazil will have access to it is cause for celebration.

Let's return to that 2013 study showing that half of the people who sign up for these online classes are doing so not just for a specific professional purpose. We see the same phenomenon in the explosion of interest in adult learning courses, books, and videos. Why are all these people around the world signing up for courses in art history and psychology and physics? If it doesn't help them get a job, why do they want to know this stuff?

5

Knowledge and Power

IF IGNORANCE IS bliss, why do people want knowledge? This is a question with a long pedigree in Western culture. Prometheus brought fire from Mount Olympus down to earth and its mortal inhabitants. In doing so, he enraged Zeus, the supreme deity, who had him chained to a rock and tortured for eternity by an eagle feasting on his liver. And that was just the punishment for Prometheus. Human beings were sent a curse in the form of Pandora, with her box of ills that would afflict humankind forever once it was unlocked—disease, sickness, sorrow, envy, hatred.

Prometheus's fire may have been a metaphor for knowledge. In Aeschylus's version of the legend, in addition to the burning branch, Prometheus introduced humans to the arts, including writing, mathematics, astronomy, architecture, and medicine. In other words, Prometheus decided to bring a liberal arts curriculum down from the heavens—and he and all of humankind paid a dreadful price for it.

So did Adam and Eve. The story at the heart of biblical history is about the dangers of knowledge. According to Genesis, there were many trees in the Garden of Eden, but only two had names: the Tree of Life and the Tree of Knowledge. God forbade Adam and Eve from eating the fruit of the latter, warning that if they did, they would die.* The serpent, representing Satan, told the couple not to be timid, assuring them that eating the fruit would not result in death. God didn't want them to eat it, the serpent told Eve, because if they did, "your eyes shall be opened, and ye shall be as Gods, knowing good and evil."

So Adam and Eve plucked the fruit and ate it. When God realized what they had done, he was mer-

---

* There are those who argue that the tree is really an arbitrary sign of obedience. But as the Milton scholar David Scott Kastan notes in his introduction to *Paradise Lost* (Indianapolis: Hackett, 2005), xlv, why then is it not called the "Tree of Obedience"? The forbidden fruit of knowledge is clearly central to the story.

ciless in his punishment. He told Eve, "I will greatly multiply thy sorrow and thy conception," and then condemned women for eternity to the pains of childbirth. He told Adam, "Cursed is the ground for thy sake; in sorrow shalt thou eat of it all the days of thy life." And, of course, he banished them from the Garden of Eden. In other words, human beings came to earth as fallen creatures, born in original sin, because they desired knowledge.

This notion that knowledge is dangerous has recurred in Western thought for millennia. Given that the West has made such great strides in its understanding of the universe, it is interesting to note that non-Western cultures do not have equivalent myths about the perils of learning. There are some similar stories in other civilizations, but nothing with the import of the tale of Prometheus or the biblical fall of man. Perhaps it is because the West has been so persistently inquisitive that it has also been fearful of the consequences of its curiosity.

The phrase "ignorance is bliss" comes from a beautiful poem, "Ode on a Distant Prospect of Eton College," by the eighteenth-century English writer Thomas Gray. In it, the poet writes of his return to his old school and is delighted to see the "happy hills, . . . redolent of joy and youth." He conjures up a bucolic fantasy of innocent pleasures. But he then thinks about all the bad things that are in store for these young men in the real world once they leave the cloistered environment of Eton—fear, jealousy, anger, despair, poverty, death, and "Sorrow's piercing dart." It's better that they not be made aware of these realities. "Thought would destroy their paradise," he concludes, "where ignorance is bliss, / 'Tis folly to be wise."

And yet, despite the danger, despite the sorrow, we keep asking questions and searching for answers. Cicero believed that it was in our nature to be "drawn to the pursuit of knowledge." Many modern biologists concur, arguing that the core of being human involves the use of the brain. More than three million years ago, our ancestors began to walk on their hind legs. That freed their hands to do other things and, most significantly, coincided with the growth of the human brain. The big brain is the single largest point of differentiation between human beings and other animals. Richard Dawkins explains why:

> Other species can communicate, but no other species has true language with open-ended grammar. No other species has literature, music, art, mathematics or science. No other species makes books, or complicated machines such as cars, computers and combine har-

vesters. No other species devotes substantial lengths of time to pursuits that don't contribute directly to survival or reproduction.

In the beginning, before we humans were writing operas and making iPads, our ancestors combined their brain power with their hands—now free from the task of walking—to forage for food and make simple tools. They used their primitive mental capacity to find ways to improve their circumstances in the natural environment rather than simply adapting to them like all other animals. As Jacob Bronowski wrote in *The Ascent of Man*, man became "a singular creature . . . not a figure in the landscape" but "a shaper of the landscape." Humans sought ways to control their environment and thus became hunter-gatherers, farmers, warriors, and, eventually, builders of cities and states, of civilizations.

At the heart of farming and building was the search for knowledge, but of a practical kind. The ancient Greeks were the first to try to understand the world in an abstract sense. They called such an exploration *philosophy*, which means "love of wisdom." This involved understanding not only human nature but also nature itself. The latter exploration they called "natural philosophy"—which much later became known as science. Over time, a divide grew between the study of human beings and the study of nature. The former seemed soft and speculative, the latter hard and definitive. Bertrand Russell, the early-twentieth-century scientist and philosopher, once pithily described the difference between science and philosophy. "Science," he explained, "is what we know, and philosophy is what we don't know." In this view, philosophy involves speculations about things of which one cannot have definite proof. Once you gain certainty about a particular subject, it moves from the realm of philosophy to science. For Russell, philosophy was immensely important because there was a vast array of things one did not know much about and perhaps could not know much about. But philosophy still was, in his phrase, "incomplete science." The word *science*, after all, comes from the Latin word for "to know."

Russell's notion of philosophy as a precursor to science makes some sense historically. Human beings wondered why the sun rose or the tides came in, and speculated that there were divine spirits behind them. The Greeks posited all kinds of causes for natural phenomena, often attributing them to gods and goddesses, but also to physical and biological factors. Over the course of centuries, scientific inquiry—theorizing, experimentation, observation—rejected, corrected, and amended many of these theories. We no longer think that there are spirits in trees, that the Sun God rides his chariot across the skies every day, or that female embryos are created due to a "deficiency of heat" in the body (Aristotle's explanation). We no longer think that the earth is flat or that it is at the center of the universe, two views that were widespread among learned scholars for centuries. Science replaced philosophy, in Russell's terms.

The search for knowledge gave human beings power, just as the Bible anticipated, and that power has been used for good and ill. But on the whole, there has been a steady and persistent effort to improve human life. Progress in technology and medicine certainly has dark side effects—the dangers of nuclear war, the impact of economic growth on the environment, the moral dilemmas of cloning. Over the last five hundred years, however, the consequences of knowledge have been positive, and over the last two hundred, staggeringly positive. At the most basic level, people enjoy longer and healthier lives, possess greater material prosperity, and are organized in ways that have reduced cruelty and misery.

Just as a reminder of what scientific progress means for humans, here is a brief account of how one of the most powerful men of the seventeenth century, Charles II of England, was treated after he had a mild stroke in 1685 (from which he almost certainly would have recovered on his own). His fourteen physicians, the best in the land, began by bleeding him, taking a pint of blood. The king's chief physician decided they had not gone far enough and removed an extra eight ounces by cutting into the king's shoulders. Vomiting was induced and purgatives and enemas delivered. Charles regained consciousness, but over the next five days, his physicians continued to administer enemas and bleedings. He was given sneezing powder, forced to drink various potions, and his feet were smeared with pigeon dung. Finally, after an antidote containing "extracts of all the herbs and animals of the kingdom" was forced down his throat (according to his physician's journal), the king died. And that was the world's finest health care at the time.

Life expectancy around the time of Charles II was about thirty years, and it remained roughly the same until 1900. Life expectancy today is seventy years for the world population as a whole, and higher for people in advanced countries. Recent material progress has been astonishing. Before the turn of the millennium, the United Nations estimated that global poverty had declined more in the second half of the twentieth century than in the prior five hundred years. The average Chinese person today is forty times richer and lives thirty years longer than he or she did fifty years ago. China's progress is the most remarkable, but it is widely shared. In 1960, nearly one in five children died. Today the ratio is one in twenty. It is quite possible that extreme poverty—life on less than $1.25 a day—will be extinct in a generation.

These numbers are seen mostly as a testament to scientific knowledge. And, of course, it's self-evident that medicine, vaccines, and hygiene have all contributed mightily to the improvements. But the softer sciences and humanities have also yielded powerful benefits. Human beings have organized themselves in more productive ways, economically, politically, and socially. And these changes in organization and behavior have been the result of better ideas, sometimes arrived at through speculation and insight, though mostly through trial and error—which is the only way that experiments in social science can take place in the real world.

In his book *The Rational Optimist*, Matt Ridley notes that over time, human beings learned that open exchanges—of ideas, goods, and services—produced powerful benefits for all. He also explains that the rise of specialization, or the division of labor, increased economic output across the globe. Ideas like these were adopted haltingly, with many steps taken backward as well as forward as the unsuccessful copied the successful. In *The Better Angels of Our Nature*, Steven Pinker makes the now famous claim that we are living in the most peaceful time in human history. He argues that the rise of certain ideas has had a powerful, beneficial impact on the world. The Enlightenment concepts of individual liberty, autonomy, and dignity, for instance, and the beginning of a "humanitarian revolution" transformed the world by ending practices like slavery. Pinker also writes about the more recent "rights revolutions," which have led to less cruelty toward minorities, women, gays, and others who were not at the center of the old power structures of society.

Some humanists balk at the idea that human beings have made any progress in these fundamental ways. Are we better off than the ancient Greeks? they might ask. The answer is yes, overwhelmingly, unless you were one of the handful of male Greek aristocrats (and even then, as long as you didn't get a toothache). Practices like slavery, serfdom, dueling, and the abuse of women and children have dwindled over the last few centuries—as a consequence of broad, humanistic ideas, the bedrock of a liberal education. To be sure, more progress is needed, and in some cases, new and perverse forms of oppression have replaced the old-fashioned, easily identifiable ones. But that cannot negate the reality that knowledge has led to human advances in tangible ways.

Four hundred years ago, absolute monarchs governed much of the world, and the vast majority of the human population possessed little economic and political freedom. Today, most people live in democracies, and whatever their flaws, they are usually better than the rapacious dictatorships of the past. Until recently, a country's economic policies were designed to produce the maximum benefit for a tiny elite. Think of Africa in the nineteenth century, where whole nations were turned into regions of slave labor and economic extraction, to benefit a small number of Europeans. What followed after decolonization in the 1950s were local dictators who were equally brutal and rapacious. Today, Africa is still home to some dictatorships and faces rampant corruption in certain areas. But compared with three decades ago—or a century ago—there has been significant progress along almost every political, economic, and social measure.

The fundamental reason for the rise of the rest—the fact that developing countries are growing much faster than in decades past—has to do with the diffusion of knowledge. When I visit developing countries, nearly everywhere I find they are run more effectively today than they were decades ago. Those at the helm of economic policy are almost invariably graduates of programs in economics from Western universities. They studied at, say, the University of Chicago, or Georgetown, or the London School of Economics, and then returned to their central banks and finance ministries to implement some of what they had learned. Health care is being provided in a more systematic and thoughtful way, based on ideas that have been tried and proved elsewhere. These kinds of policies are reinforced by a broader culture of educational exchange that takes place through conferences, meetings, publications, and televised conversation. It's not perfect by any means, but it's a lot better than it was thirty years ago.

Social science is not science—because, as the Nobel Prize–winning economist Herbert Simon put it, "the subjects of our study think"—but some academic learning has been applied in the real world. Governments have come to adopt best practices from the social sciences, though there are limits to progress in fields as messy as economics and political science. Even steps forward produce a host of unintended consequences that have to be dealt with. Advanced industrial countries continue to face many problems today. Yet consider their expansive ambitions: to provide economic growth and social security for every one of their citizens. Governments have never tried to do so much for so many.

Knowledge can be used for terrible purposes. Fascism, communism, and Islamic fundamentalism have all managed to weave a dangerous ideology out of elements of knowledge. But people have always sought power, and some of them have justified that pursuit through bad ideas. These ideas, in almost all such cases, are covers for power grabs. That's not to say that ideas do not have a life of their own. Nationalism and religion can be powerful ideologies that hold societies together and stir human beings to action, even horrific violence. But historically, this has not been enough to produce real success, the kind that produces long-term trends in a society's favor. Governments organized around bad political and economic ideas have required force, coercion, and bribery to succeed—and these are difficult to sustain. Countries like Nazi Germany and Soviet Russia failed because other countries, such as the United States, opposed them. And free societies like America prevailed in large part because they had greater staying power, because their organizing ideas were superior. U.S. strategy might have been better than Germany's and the Soviet Union's in World War II and the Cold War, but the real cause of victory was the ability of the U.S. economy to outproduce the Nazi and Soviet economies. In the long run, societies based on submission generally find themselves at odds with natural human impulses. The ones that have succeeded in some fashion, like China, have actually allowed a great deal of freedom and autonomy in several spheres of society while maintaining control in others. The more China opens itself up to a broad exploration of knowledge, to humanistic ideas, to open exchanges—in other words, the values that liberal education celebrates—the more the government will struggle to maintain its tight political control.

The *New York Times* columnist Nicholas Kristof has pointed to three ideas associated with the humanities that have positively shaped the world. First, he notes the philosopher Isaiah Berlin's warning that the belief in a single, all-encompassing truth inevitably produces blind arrogance, possibly leading to dangerous consequences. Second, he highlights John Rawls's contribution to political thought: that the most just society would be the one you would choose if you did not know how rich or poor or how talented or untalented you were when born into it. Since those are often matters of genetics and luck, Rawls posited that we should judge a society from behind this "veil of ignorance." Lastly, Kristof highlights the work of Peter

Singer, who has brought the treatment of animals and the pain that human beings often needlessly cause them to the fore of our moral consciousness. These are just a few examples. There are many other ideas in the social sciences and humanities that represent, in some way or another, an accumulation of knowledge and a growth in insight marking an advance in human affairs.

Of course, most people read books, understand science, and experience art, not to change the world, but to change themselves. But is our current system of liberal education changing young people for the better?

6

In Defense of
Today's Youth

ONE OF THE enduring benefits of a liberal education is that it broadens us. When we absorb great
literature, we come face to face with ideas, experiences, and emotions that we might never otherwise
encounter in our lifetime. When we read history,
we encounter people from a different age and learn
from their triumphs and travails. When we study
physics and biology, we comprehend the mysteries
of the universe and human life. And when we listen
to great music, we are moved in ways that reason
cannot comprehend. This may not help make a living, but it will help make a life. We all play many

roles, professional and personal, in one lifetime. A liberal education gives us a greater capacity to be good workers, but it will also give us the capacity to be good partners, friends, parents, and citizens.

Does a liberal education make us better human beings? Students at colleges and universities certainly get a high-quality, expensive education as preparation to succeed in the outside world. But, according to many critics, even the best students—and sometimes especially the best—are limited in crucial ways. To put it bluntly, the charge is that they are achievement-oriented automatons, focused on themselves and their careers. They do not seem interested in delving deep into the search for inner knowledge, giving reign to their passions, or developing their character. The "Me Generation" was the name given to the baby boomers. *Time* magazine ran a cover in 2013 on the millennials with the title "The Me Me Me Generation."

In early 2001, the columnist David Brooks wrote a now famous essay in the *Atlantic* titled "The Organization Kid," based on days of meetings he had with students and professors during a visit to Princeton University. In the essay, Brooks described the next generation of American leaders and their daily schedule: "Crew practice at dawn, classes in the morning, resident-adviser duty, lunch, study groups, classes in the afternoon, tutoring disadvantaged kids in Trenton, a cappella practice, dinner, study, science lab, prayer session, hit the StairMaster, study a few hours more." It's an impressive list, but Brooks found that this intense set of activities was mostly in the service of building a resume and came with little intellectual curiosity. Even more noticeable, to him, was the total lack of desire to think about moral issues, to be introspective, or to focus on the building of character or virtue. In the end, he concluded:

> At the top of the meritocratic ladder we have in America a generation of students who are extraordinarily bright, morally earnest, and incredibly industrious. They like to study and socialize in groups. They create and join organizations with great enthusiasm. They are responsible, safety-conscious, and mature. They feel no compelling need to rebel—not even a hint of one. They not only defer to authority; they admire it. "Alienation" is a word one almost never hears from them. They regard the universe as beneficent, orderly, and meaningful. At the schools and colleges where the next leadership class is being bred, one finds not angry revolutionaries, despondent slackers, or dark cynics but the Organization Kid.

In 2014, the essayist William Deresiewicz stepped up the criticism with his book *Excellent Sheep: The*

Miseducation of the American Elite and the Way to a Meaningful Life. In it, Deresiewicz recounts his experiences teaching undergraduates at Yale and describes them as having spent their lives getting ready to attend elite colleges but lacking any sense of direction once they arrived. They had jumped through one hurdle after another in order to get a liberal education, but they didn't know what to do with it once they had their degree. As a result, Deresiewicz finds them to be privileged—"entitled little shit[s]" is the phrase he uses—but intellectually and morally uncurious, uninterested in exploring the larger questions about the meaning of life, and unwilling to take intellectual risks. They are comfortably bourgeois and achievement oriented, but they care little about the inner self and the soul.

The notion that young people are somehow callow and morally unserious is not a new charge. In 700 BC, the Greek poet Hesiod wrote about it. The philosophers Xenophon and Plato were dismayed by the moral decay of their youth. The Romans saw loss of virtue all around them. The Victorians decried the decline in religiosity in the next generation. And while America has always been different—born new, focused on the future, itself an experiment in modernity—it has had its own tradition of jeremiads. From the Puritans to Henry David Thoreau, to conservatives horrified by the 1960s, to Christopher Lasch, who wrote *The Culture of Narcissism* in 1979, they all worried about a new generation that was less interested in community and more interested in itself.

The most recent round of critiques began with the conservative intellectual Allan Bloom and the publication of his 1987 book, *The Closing of the American Mind*. But since then, conservatives and liberals have jumped in with equal fervor. Brooks, Deresiewicz, and Anthony Kronman, former dean of the Yale Law School, have all joined the chorus, sounding a similar, plaintive tone. But most of the complaints today are quite different from the reactionary concerns of the past. After centuries of bemoaning the fact that the young are too rebellious and disrespectful, the problem today, it appears, is that they are not rebellious and disrespectful enough. They aren't willing to challenge conventional wisdom, neither the liberal pieties that offended Allan Bloom nor the conservative ones that gall Deresiewicz. After having been pilloried for trying to destroy the bourgeois order in the 1960s and 1970s, the youth are now scorned for being too bourgeois. Too many young people, it seems, are well adjusted, responsible, and looking for good jobs. If only they would wander off campus and study tantric rituals, smoke pot and read Hegel, and stage a sit-in or two—then they would show us their inner souls. (Of course, imagine the reaction of many of the same critics were the college students actually to do that!) You can't help but sympathize with the sophomore who said to me, "I think that whatever we did, we would be falling short by some measure—and people would write about that."

In fact, the picture that the critics paint certainly does ring true in its focus on the culture of achievement that dominates student lives at the top educational institutions today. But it's strange to blame the students for something that is largely beyond their control. After all, they did not devise the intense system of tests that comprise the gateway to American higher education, nor did they create the highly competitive job market in anxious economic times. Admissions offices now prize nothing less than perfection. I once asked the head of admissions at an Ivy League college, "Do you take in many kids who have failed in some significant way in high school?" He immediately answered, "No, that would place them at a disadvantage compared with others with better records." I pointed out that how one responds to and recovers from failure is one of the most important characteristics of an individual, probably one that reveals more about his or her future success. The admissions officer, a deeply educated scholar, said he understood, but noted that if he admitted kids who had failed in some way—with transcripts and SAT scores reflecting this failure—the college would drop in its rankings and its "win-loss ratio" against other key schools (that is the percentage of students who, when admitted to two schools, accept one over the other). The pressure is intense, for the colleges and the kids. Is it such a wonder that students respond as they do?

The pressure doesn't stop once they get into college. The race continues with markers set up to point them toward summer jobs, internships, and fellowships, and finally full-time jobs. The process of getting hired at a prestigious bank or consulting firm now involves a marathon of interviews and examinations, with thousands applying for the few positions on offer. But the critics seem to feel that in confronting this grueling system of rewards, kids should take it easy, relax, follow their bliss, and search for their souls. Apparently, Goldman Sachs will understand.

Moreover, students' focus on achievement has not, so far as I can tell, produced young men and women who are, in some way, mean, selfish, or cruel. There's really no evidence for this at all. They are probably less bigoted, racist, and sexist than prior generations of students, something that's easy to caricature as political correctness but is admirable nonetheless, especially if you're a minority, a woman, or gay. I have spent time on college campuses and around young people, and certainly I find them to be thoughtful, interesting, and stimulating. Professor Steven Pinker, who has spent much more time with college students (teaching them), has written in the same vein. But these are anecdotes. Is there any evidence? In fact, there is. Since 1966, UCLA's Higher Education Research Institute (HERI) has asked incoming college freshmen a set of questions. The data collected show the following: Over the last four decades, students have become more conscious of the need to make money. But much of that change took place from 1967 to 1987, and the percentage of freshmen who identify "becoming well off financially" as a personal objective has steadied significantly since then. That's surely a rational response to an economy that has produced fewer good jobs, where the median income has flatlined, and where globalization and technology are replacing all kinds of once-privileged tasks. In such circumstances, to be concerned about one's future might be a sign of intelligence! Other life objectives that have risen in importance to students are "becoming a community leader," "helping others who are in difficulty," and, interestingly, "making a theoretical contribution to science," none of which are signs of selfishness.

The data also show that students today combine their worldly aspirations with a strong desire to do good. The numbers who volunteer for programs like the Peace Corps and AmeriCorps have risen substantially. In 2014, Teach for America received over fifty thousand applications, more than twice the number received in 2008. Many talented and highly credentialed students choose to work at nonprofits for a while. It's true that nongovernmental organizations have become cool, but that is the point. They have become cool precisely because young people today view them as a valuable and worthwhile way to spend part—or all—of their lives. As much as any generation before them that might have gone into politics and government or volunteered for war and exploration, they want to do good, change the world, and follow their principles. They just do it in an incremental, practical, best-practices kind of way—more McKinsey than Mother Teresa.

Somewhat different from "college students" are the millennials—generally the term is used for people born from 1980 to 2000. The charges against them are similar, though, and nastier. The cover story in *Time* magazine mentioned at the beginning

of this chapter, and written by its talented humor columnist Joel Stein, accuses the millennials of narcissism, entitlement, and (this is a new one) laziness. The
first charge is presented as a "cold, hard" fact. Citing
the National Institutes of Health, Stein writes, "The
incidence of narcissistic personality disorder is nearly
three times as high for people in their twenties as for
the generation that's now 65 or older." But as the journalist Elspeth Reeve has pointed out, this finding is
disputed by other scholars who argue that the research
merely shows all young people tend to be somewhat
narcissistic but that the narcissism fades over time—
for all. Or, to quote from the 2010 study that Reeve
cites, "First, we show that when new data on narcissism are folded into preexisting meta-analytic data,
there is no increase in narcissism in college students
over the last few decades." As for slothfulness, there is
really no evidence for this at all. The basic problem for
American workers of all ages has been that their hours
and productivity keep rising but their wages do not.

A 2014 Nielsen report, *Millennials: Breaking the
Myths*, offers some data on the generation's attitude
toward volunteering. In 2011, 75 percent made a dona-
tion to a charity, 71 percent raised money for one, and
57 percent volunteered, "more than any other generation." The three causes they care the most about,

according to the report, are education, poverty, and the environment. A study of the group sponsored by the Case Foundation, also in 2014, came to very similar conclusions. Of the 87 percent of millennials who had donated to a nonprofit, more than half had given more than one hundred dollars. In a "TED Talk" explaining the behavior of millennials, marketing expert Scott Hess contrasts them with their predecessors, "Generation X." Instead of being "slackers," "judgmental," and "anti-corporate," he said, millennials are "leaning forward," "engaged," "inclusive," and "tolerant," and they believe that "commerce" can be "lubricated by conscience." And unlike generations right before them, they don't view their parents as adversaries but rather as friends and helpers. Perhaps I say this because I'm a parent, but is this so terrible?

A constant refrain one hears about the young, whether millennials or students or young workers, is that they are utterly focused on themselves. They set up their own Facebook pages, tweet, and send pictures of themselves eating or playing sports. In a talk at Princeton in November 2012, David Brooks praised the self-abnegation of General George Marshall, who refused to ask for command of Operation Overlord—the D-day invasion of Europe—because he thought it would be self-serving. I love that story about Marshall myself, but I also recognize that he lived in a different age. Those were times when large institutions—private and public—dominated life. They were powerful and stable, and they looked after individuals for their entire careers. Your task was to fit in, to put the interest of the institution above your own, to be a good team player. Then you would be rewarded with security and success. (Marshall *was* subsequently appointed secretary of state, then secretary of defense.) Today, everyone is told, that compact has been broken. Everything is in flux. You must be entrepreneurial and recognize that you will need to change jobs and even careers over a lifetime. No company will stay loyal to you, nor can you lock yourself into one place. The billionaire-founder of LinkedIn, Reid Hoffman, wrote a book titled *The Start-up of You: Adapt to the Future, Invest in Yourself, and Transform Your Career*, to explain how to succeed in today's world. The ultimate irony, surely, is that the very commentators who are urging young Americans to be less self-obsessed are busily building their own personal brands, complete with websites, Facebook pages, and Twitter accounts. If it's right for them, why is it not right for everyone else?

Some things the young don't do. In general, political activism on campuses has declined in recent decades—despite spikes during the first Reagan and

Obama campaigns. But that lack of enthusiasm for politics again reflects a broader social trend. Most Americans are deeply disenchanted with politics. Younger Americans believe that the U.S. government has become dysfunctional and polarized. The young might choose to effect social change by working with NGOs rather than working for government, but that is about the mechanism not the goal. And given the state of politics, the bureaucracy of government, and the intrusions of a hyperactive media, surely they are being rational, maybe even wise.

Perhaps the most striking result from the HERI survey involves the broadest issue: the number of incoming freshmen who consider "developing a meaningful philosophy of life" essential or very important has plummeted from 86 percent in 1967 to 45 percent in 2013. That number is probably what Brooks, Deresiewicz, and others are describing in richer detail in their portrayals of college campuses today. And it makes them worried about the present and nostalgic for an earlier age.

I understand the nostalgia. Today's students don't seem as animated by big arguments as generations of the past did. They don't make big speeches about grand philosophical issues. They don't stay up late arguing about Nietzsche or Marx or Tolstoy. But that is part of the tenor of the times, something students reflect rather than create. When I was growing up, the Cold War was raging, and that meant there was a great contest of ideas taking place around the world. People wondered whether countries such as India would go capitalist, communist, or something in between. These political ideas mattered to people— young and old—and had huge consequences. And the political ideas, in turn, rested on large philosophical ideas about the nature of human beings and societies. I arrived at college in 1982, which, it turned out, coincided with the last gasp of the ideological battle that had dominated the twentieth century. Ronald Reagan had come to power and had called the Soviet Union an evil empire. The Soviets were still on the march in much of the Third World. Communism and capitalism were still ideas in battle around the world.

My friends and I would sit around in coffee shops and passionately debate the American nuclear buildup, the proxy war in Central America, Reagan's and Thatcher's policies. The divisions were deep, the answers were unknown, and the consequences were believed to be huge. In 1983, ABC aired a television movie called *The Day After*, dramatizing what life in America would look like in the wake of a nuclear war. It ran for two hours in prime time and was followed by an interview of then secretary of state George Shultz and a long discussion including Henry Kissinger, Elie Weisel, Carl Sagan, William Buckley, and Robert McNamara. For weeks afterward, people talked about the movie and the politics and ethics involved in making it. College students were deeply engaged by these kinds of events. They marched by the thousands over the divestment campaign against South Africa, American support for the contras in Nicaragua, and the nuclear freeze. But it all emanated from that central philosophical-political contest of ideas between communism and capitalism, Leninism and democracy.

We live in a very different age today, one in which there are fewer grand ideological debates with great consequences. It is inconceivable that anything like *The Day After* would be made, let alone trigger much discussion. Islamic terrorism is a security threat and did provoke some debate after 9/11, but it has limited potency and certainly has no chance of seducing a non-Muslim country. Even in Muslim countries, jihadists have to resort to terror precisely because they can convince only a small band of extremists of the strength of their ideas. They pose a threat but not an ideological threat. We have noisy partisanship in Washington, but over fairly routine political differences. On issues, both parties are actually much closer than they were thirty or forty years ago. As a result, our youth are not very ideological. They combine a mix of impulses—capitalist, socially liberal, supportive of social welfare, but uncomfortable with bureaucracy and regulation. It doesn't quite add up to a passionate political philosophy. And certainly, it doesn't take them to the barricades.

Our age is defined by capitalism, globalization, and technology. The trends changing life come from those forces—powering a new information revolution that creates new industries overnight, pushing the frontiers of computer learning, changing medicine in fundamental ways, allowing billions to rise in China and India, and altering the structures of economic, political, and social power everywhere. The icons of the age are entrepreneurs, technologists, and businesspeople. Mark Zuckerberg and Jeff Bezos are far more important symbols than any politician today, and they occupy the space that iconic political figures did in earlier eras. The young reflect today's realities. Their lives are more involved with these economic and technological forces than with ideology and geopolitics. And that means there is less scope for grand theorizing, fewer intense late-night bull sessions, less stirring eloquence at the student forums and political unions. It's a new world, and the young know it.

But is this so bad? Are the issues that students today think about less important than those of war and peace? Are their heroes inferior to those of past ages? The geeky culture of the technology era is less conspicuously interested in ideas than Cold War society was, with its great statesmen and philosophers. But is it any worse? Consider Bill Gates, perhaps too old now to be sexy but certainly the iconic figure of this age. A technology entrepreneur and businessman, Gates was one of the first larger-than-life private figures in contemporary America. He is informal, brainy, merit oriented, and seemingly uninterested in showing off his wealth. On the whole, these are great values to transmit. Gates is also deeply interested in ideas that range from science to economics to education. His speeches and blog posts are filled with discussions of books, including arguments, analyses, and data about them. His kind of wonkery may not look like a grand exercise in philosophy, but he is actively engaged with important ideas that could change the world.

More important, his main handiwork now, the Bill & Melinda Gates Foundation, sees its central mission as saving the largest number of human lives it can, no matter where they live, what color their skin is, or what passport they carry. In other words, it is built on an idea, that all human life is of equal value, something only a few charities believe in or act on. This might once have been considered a Christian idea—that we are all equal in God's eyes—but Gates has translated it into a secular one, and he is giving away the world's largest fortune in service of it. His friend Warren Buffett, the second-richest man in America, is giving away most of his wealth to the same cause—without asking for any credit, not even to have his name put on the foundation's door. (That is surely an act that bears some similarity to Marshall's modesty.)

In his writings and talks, David Brooks emphasizes his concern that the young lack a language about virtue today. They are, he believes, "morally inarticulate." And it's true that we don't use words like *honorable*, *noble*, and *virtuous* much these days, but surely that is how Gates's and Buffett's actions should be described. They are examples of people who have been moved to take large, important actions out of deep convictions, ideas, and values—out of a philosophy of life and a commitment to those ideas. Their model is surely as inspiring as any statesman or general of the past who spoke in lofty tones about good and evil, honor and sacrifice.

Not everyone can do what Gates and Buffett are doing. College students today search for morality and the meaning of life in different ways than in prior ages, as with any new generation, especially in times of tremendous change. They are more incremental and practical. They seek truth, but perhaps through quieter avenues than the heroic ones of the past. They try to combine their great urges with a good life.

The HERI survey data show that the objective most important to students, besides making money, is raising a family. That number has been remarkably stable over the years, rising somewhat, and is now around 75 percent. It's a bourgeois concern. But is there really something soulless about trying to make a living, create a home, and raise a family? One of the higher achievements of the liberal democratic project is surely that people today can spend less time worrying about revolution and war and focus instead on building a private sphere within which they can find meaning, fulfillment, and happiness. I remember reading once about a judge in South Africa who spoke to American college students. She contrasted the high-stakes politics in her country—the breakdown of apartheid, the birth of a new country—with the trivia she read about in American newspapers. And she concluded by fervently hoping that one day her country would be normal enough to have its papers filled with trivia.

There are plenty of challenges abroad and at home,

injustice and imbalances that need to be corrected and reformed. But there are also those times and places where people are lucky enough that private virtues might be cultivated. As John Adams famously wrote during the American Revolution, "I must study politics and war, that our sons may have liberty to study mathematics and philosophy. Our sons ought to study mathematics and philosophy, geography, natural history and naval architecture, navigation, commerce and agriculture in order to give their children a right to study painting, poetry, music, architecture, statuary, tapestry and porcelain." So maybe today they're writing apps rather than studying poetry, but that's an adjustment for the age.

These are not the sorts of ambitions that have people rallying to the ramparts and declaiming in purple prose, but they are still real and authentic and important. And they are worth a brief defense, which is what I have attempted here. This much I will concede: Because of the times we live in, all of us, young and old, do not spend enough time and effort thinking about the meaning of life. We do not look inside of ourselves enough to understand our strengths and weaknesses, and we do not look around enough—at the world, in history—to ask the deepest and broadest questions. The solution surely is that, even now, we could all use a little bit more of a liberal education.

Notes

Liberal education is a topic on which many excellent books have been written. I have used a few footnotes in the text to highlight particular works on which I relied for some historical background. The rest of my sources are acknowledged in these endnotes.

1: Coming to America

16 As college enrollment has grown: U.S. Department of Education, National Center for Education Statistics, *Digest of Education Statistics 2013*, Table 322.10. The *Digest*, published annually by the National Center for Education Statistics, is a highly accessible source for statistics on higher education. The data are updated throughout the year online at http://nces.ed.gov/programs/digest/.

16 in earlier periods of educational expansion: For more on the post–World War II expansion in higher education and the simultaneous rise in the humanities, see Louis Menand, "The Humanities Revolution,"

in *The Marketplace of Ideas: Reform and Resistance in the American University* (New York: W. W. Norton, 2010), 63–73; and William M. Chace, "The Decline of the English Department," *American Scholar*, Autumn 2009. The Humanities Indicators, a project of the American Academy of Arts and Sciences available online at www.humanitiesindicators.org, also tracks data on the twentieth-century rise and fall in the study of the humanities.

17 "I have to speak": Philip Roth, *Portnoy's Complaint* (New York: Vintage Books, 1994), 164.

17 Here are the data: National Center for Education Statistics, *Digest*, Table 311.60.

18 Another estimate: Measures of the liberal arts vary by source, depending largely on how academic fields are classified. Justin Pope, "Liberal Arts Colleges Forced to Evolve with Market," Associated Press, Dec. 30, 2012, estimates that between 100,000 and 300,000 of the country's approximately 17 million undergraduates attend a liberal arts college, that is, a residential college that exists independent of any larger university. The same article estimates that about one-third of bachelor's degrees in the United States are awarded in the liberal arts.

The *Digest* places the undergraduate population at 18 million as of 2012 (Table 303.60). It also divides degrees into six broad categories: humanities; social and behavioral sciences; natural sciences and mathematics; computer sciences and engineering; education; business; and other fields, a category that includes professional programs such as agriculture and law enforcement. If just the first three are classified as liberal, then about 40 percent of the 1.8 million bachelor's degrees conferred in 2011–12 were in the liberal arts (Table 318.20).

19 governors: See Scott Jaschik, "Florida GOP vs. Social Science," *Inside Higher Ed*, Oct. 12, 2011 (Scott quote); Kevin Kiley, "A $10,000 Platform," *Inside Higher Ed*, Nov. 30, 2012; and Kiley, "Another Liberal Arts Critic," *Inside Higher Ed*, Jan. 30, 2013 (Bennett quote).

19 It isn't only Republicans: Scott Jaschik, "Apology from Obama," *Inside Higher Ed*, Feb. 19, 2014.

20 their comprehensive study of education: Claudia Goldin and Lawrence Katz, *The Race between Education and Technology* (Cambridge: Harvard University Press, 2010), 28–29.

21 Today a high school student: Ibid., 254.

22 Jawaharlal Nehru: On Nehru's economic views, see Shashi Tharoor, *Nehru: The Invention of India* (New York: Arcade, 2003), 159–193; and Jawaharlal Nehru, "Temples of the New Age," July 8, 1954, available at http://www.nehruinternationalconference2014.com/ nehru_speech4.aspx.

30 "The Other America": Fatma Zakaria, "The Other America," *Times of India*, Mar. 28, 1982.

2: A Brief History of Liberal Education

40 Prior to the change: Bruce Kimball, *Orators and Philosophers: A History of the Idea of Liberal Education* (New York: Teachers College Press, 1986), 16–17. Kimball's book is a detailed, scholarly history of liberal education from antiquity through the modern era. Also see Werner Jaeger's seminal work on the development of culture and education in ancient

Greece: *Paideia: The Ideals of Greek Culture*, trans. Gilbert Highet, 3 vols. (Oxford, UK: Oxford University Press, 1939–1944).

41 "Our constitution": Thucydides, *History of the Peloponnesian War*, trans. Rex Warner (New York: Penguin, 1954), 2.37.

42 "Learning will spoil": Frederick Douglass, *The Life and Times of Frederick Douglass* (1881), in *Autobiographies* (New York: Library of America, 1994), 527. Also quoted in Michael Roth, *Beyond the University: Why Liberal Education Matters* (New Haven, CT: Yale University Press, 2014), 42.

42 intellectual disagreement: This is the argument Kimball makes in his book—that liberal education represents two traditions, that of the orators and that of the philosophers.

42 first great divide: See Werner Jaeger, "The Rhetoric of Isocrates and Its Cultural Ideal," in *Paideia*, vol. 3: 46–70.

43 one of the earliest writers: Kimball, *Orators and Philosophers*, 13.

43 "For it is from knowledge": Cicero, *On the Orator, Books 1–2*, trans. E. W. Sutton and H. Rackham (Loeb Classical Library No. 348) (Cambridge, MA: Harvard University Press, 1942), 1.20.

44 "finally and definitively formalized": Paul Abelson, *The Seven Liberal Arts: A Study in Medieval Culture* (New York: Russell & Russell, 1965), 2.

44 Charlemagne then established: Kimball, *Orators and Philosophers*, 51–52.

45 Why did European learning: For more on the Islamic influence, see Toby E. Huff, *The Rise of*

Early Modern Science: Islam, China, and the West, 2nd ed. (Cambridge, UK: Cambridge University Press, 2003), 47–89, 149–179. Also see Michael H. Shank, *The Scientific Enterprise in Antiquity and the Middle Ages* (Chicago: University of Chicago Press, 1996), 215–231.

46 "nations": Entry for "nation," in *Encyclopedia Britannica*, Encyclopedia Britannica Online Academic Edition (Encyclopedia Britannica, 2014).

46 By 1300, western Europe was home: Kimball, *Orators and Philosophers*, 75.

47 "revival of arts and of letters": Paul Oskar Kristeller, "Humanism," *Minerva* 16, no. 4 (Winter 1978): 586.

47 "college as we know it": Andrew Delbanco, *College: What It Was, Is, and Should Be* (Princeton, NJ: Princeton University Press, 2012), 36–37. Also, for a smart collection of thoughts on education, written in the 1950s but surprisingly current, see A. Whitney Griswold, *Liberal Education and the Democratic Ideal: And Other Essays* (New Haven, CT: Yale University Press, 1962). For a more a discursive but wide set of reflections, see Michael Oakeshott, *The Voice of Liberal Learning* (New Haven, CT: Yale University Press, 1990).

48 public lecture: Delbanco, *College*, 61–62.

48 more secular: Yale-NUS College, *Yale-NUS College: A New Community of Learning, a Report Submitted by the Inaugural Curriculum Committee of Yale-NUS College* (New Haven, CT, April 2013), 12–13, available at http://www.yale-nus.edu.sg/wp-content/uploads/2013/09/Yale-NUS-College-Curriculum-Report.pdf.

49 "lateral learning": See Delbanco, *College*, 53–56.

49 "Book learning alone": Samuel Eliot Morison, *Found-*

ing of Harvard College (Cambridge, MA: Harvard University Press, 1935), 252, quoted in Delbanco, *College*, 41–42.

50 Many of the founders: Delbanco, *College*, 39.

50 "The subject-matter of knowledge": John Henry Newman, quoted in Delbanco, *College*, 41.

51 After much deliberation: Committee of the Corporation and the Academical Faculty, *Reports on the Course of Instruction in Yale College* (New Haven, CT, 1828).

51 Yale report explained: Ibid., 14.

51 "The two great points": Ibid., 7.

52 Charles Eliot: Philo A. Hutcheson, "Eliot, Charles William," in *American National Biography Online* (Oxford University Press, Feb. 2000), available at http://www.anb.org/articles/09/09–00250.html.

53 like many other colleges: For a full account of this transition period in American higher education, see Laurence R. Veysey, *The Emergence of the American University* (Chicago: University of Chicago Press, 1965).

53 two-part essay: Charles W. Eliot, "The New Education," *Atlantic Monthly*, Feb.–Mar. 1869, the first part available at http://www.theatlantic.com/magazine/archive/1869/02/the-new-education/309049/.

54 "spontaneous diversity of choice": "Charles William Eliot," Harvard University, available at http://www.harvard.edu/history/presidents/eliot (accessed Aug. 21, 2014).

55 "Trust thyself": Ralph Waldo Emerson, "Self-Reliance," in *Essays: First Series* (1841).

55 1885 speech: Charles W. Eliot, "Liberty in Education" (speech before the Nineteenth Century Club of New York, 1885), in *Educational Reform: Essays and*

Addresses (New York: Century, 1898), 132–133, available at https://archive.org/details/educationalrefor00elioiala.

56 Eliot's views were not shared: For more on the differing views of Eliot and McCosh, see Delbanco, *College*, 82–90.

57 Against that backdrop: Louis Menand, *The Marketplace of Ideas: Reform and Resistance in the American University* (New York: W. W. Norton, 2010), 35. Less a history, this book presents an important discussion of the issues that modern universities face.

57 In 1930: See Mary Ann Dzurback, "Hutchins, Adler, and the University of Chicago: A Critical Juncture," *American Journal of Education* 99, no. 1 (1990): 64–65; and Stringfellow Barr, "A Retrospective on St. John's," *Change* 6 (1974): 35, 63.

58 Today, about 150 schools: A list of college programs that use great books, compiled by William Casement, can be found at the following Association for Core Texts and Courses (ACTC) website: http://www.coretexts.org/college-great-books-programs/ (accessed Sept. 15, 2014).

58 1952 essay: Robert M. Hutchins, "The Great Conversation" (1952), in *The Great Conversation: A Reader's Guide to Great Books of the Western World*, 2nd ed. (Chicago: Encyclopaedia Britannica, 1990), 46–73.

59 Martha Nussbaum: Martha C. Nussbaum, *Cultivating Humanity: A Classical Defense of Reform in Liberal Education* (Cambridge, MA: Harvard University Press, 1997), 33–34.

60 "Once they have gone through the Core": Delbanco, *College*, 30.

63 Grades have risen steadily: Stuart Rojstaczer and Christopher Healy, "Where A Is Ordinary: The Evolution

of American College and University Grading, 1940–2009," *Teachers College Record* 114, no. 7 (2012): 1–23.

64 portion of all grades: Brittney L. Moraski, "Report: Grade Inflation Persists," *Harvard Crimson*, May 9, 2007; Matthew Q. Clarida and Nicholas P. Fandos, "Substantiating Fears of Grade Inflation, Dean Says Median Grade at Harvard College is A–, Most Common Grade is A," *Harvard Crimson*, Dec. 4, 2013.

65 "a material universe": Anthony Kronman, *Education's End: Why Our Universities and Colleges Have Given Up on the Meaning of Life* (New Haven, CT: Yale University Press, 2007), 66.

65 "The Two Cultures": C. P. Snow, *The Two Cultures and the Scientific Revolution* (New York: Cambridge University Press, 1961).

65 "mutual incomprehension": Ibid., 15–16.

66 "A good many times": Ibid., 16.

66 In 2003, Lawrence Summers: Lawrence H. Summers, "Remarks of President Lawrence H. Summers at the Massachusetts Life Sciences Summit" (speech at the Massachusetts Life Sciences Summit, Boston, MA, Sept. 12, 2003), available at http://www.harvard.edu/president/speeches/summers_2003/lifesci.php.

66 Former Princeton president Shirley Tilghman: Shirley M. Tilghman, "The Future of Science Education in the Liberal Arts College" (speech at Presidents Institute, Council of Independent Colleges, Marco Island, FL, Jan. 5, 2010), available at http://www.princeton.edu/president/tilghman/speeches/20100105/.

67 In 2011, Yale University: Yale-NUS College, "Yale-NUS College Welcomes Inaugural Class Exceeding 150 Students," June 6, 2013, available at http://www

.yale-nus.edu.sg/newsroom/yale-nus-college-wel comes-inaugural-class-exceeding-150-students/.

68 In April 2013, a committee of this new enterprise: Yale-NUS College, *Yale-NUS College*. Since the planning stages of Yale-NUS in 2010, some Yale professors and lecturers have raised concerns about a lack of civil liberties in Singapore. See, e.g., Jim Sleeper, "Liberal Education in Authoritarian Places," *New York Times*, Aug. 31, 2013.

69 greatest innovation: Yale-NUS College, *Yale-NUS College*, 45–47.

71 In 1852, Cardinal Newman wrote: John Henry Newman, "Knowledge Its Own End," in *The Idea of a University* (London: Longmans, Green, 1907), 101–102, available at http://newmanreader.org/works/idea/dis course5.html.

71 "What is the earthly use": A. Bartlett Giamatti, "The Earthly Use of a Liberal Education," in *A Free and Ordered Space: The Real World of the University* (New York: W. W. Norton, 1990), 118–126.

3: Learning to Think

74 Bezos insists: Adam Lashinsky, "Amazon's Jeff Bezos: The Ultimate Disrupter," *Fortune*, Nov. 16, 2012. Also see Brad Stone, *The Everything Store: Jeff Bezos and the Digital Age* (New York: Little, Brown, 2013).

74 "Full sentences are harder": Lashinsky, "Amazon's Jeff Bezos."

74 "the firm I led": Norman Augustine, "One Cannot Live by Equations Alone: Education for Life and Work in

the Twenty-First Century," *Liberal Education* 99, no. 2 (Spring 2013).

75 "articulate communication": Yale-NUS College, *Yale-NUS College: A New Community of Learning, a Report Submitted by the Inaugural Curriculum Committee of Yale-NUS College* (New Haven, CT, April 2013), 25–29, available at http://www.yale-nus.edu.sg/wp-content/uploads/2013/09/Yale-NUS-College-Curriculum-Report.pdf.

77 "Conversation": A. Whitney Griswold, "On Conversation," in *Liberal Education and the Democratic Ideal: And Other Essays* (New Haven, CT: Yale University Press, 1962), 68–69.

77 "outside of the book-knowledge": Alfred North Whitehead quoted in ibid.

79 "that will help them get ready": Drew Faust quoted in Libby A. Nelson, "Gainful Employment Negotiations Wrap Up—DOJ Drops Voucher Suit—Harvard President Talks Quality, Value," *Politico*, Nov. 20, 2013.

79 Howard Gardner: Howard Gardner, *The Disciplined Mind: Beyond Facts and Standardized Tests, the K–12 Education That Every Child Deserves* (New York: Penguin, 2000).

79 "There is a joke": Ibid., 102–103.

79 Thomas Cech: Thomas R. Cech, "Science at Liberal Arts Colleges: A Better Education?" *Daedalus* 128, no. 1 (Winter 1999): 209–210. Parts of Cech's article are also quoted in Shirley M. Tilghman, "The Future of Science Education in the Liberal Arts College" (speech at Presidents Institute, Council of Independent Colleges, Marco Island, FL, Jan. 5, 2010).

80 Gardner argues: Gardner, *Disciplined Mind*, 126.

80 point of education: See the comparison Gardner draws between his views on education and those of E. D. Hirsch, an educator and proponent of "cultural literacy," in *Disciplined Mind*, 252–260.

81 "it borders on malpractice": Ibid., 260.

82 "it is in Apple's DNA": Steve Jobs quoted in Tim Carmody, "Without Jobs as CEO, Who Speaks for the Arts at Apple?" *Wired*, Aug. 29, 2011.

82 He studied ancient Greek: On Zuckerberg's interest in the classics, see Jose Antonio Vargas, "The Face of Facebook," *New Yorker*, Sept. 20, 2010.

83 "as much psychology": Mark Zuckerberg quoted in Chase Larson, "Mark Zuckerberg Speaks at BYU, Calls Facebook 'as much psychology and sociology as it is technology,'" *Deseret News*, Mar. 25, 2011.

83 "Knowledge Economy as we know it": Bruce Nussbaum, "Get Creative!" *Bloomberg Businessweek*, July 31, 2005.

84 "human tasks": David H. Autor, "Polanyi's Paradox and the Shape of Employment Growth" (paper draft dated Aug. 11, 2014, prepared for the Federal Reserve Bank of Kansas City symposium at Jackson Hole, WY, Aug. 21–23, 2014), available at http://www.kc.frb.org/publicat/sympos/2014/093014.pdf. Also see Fareed Zakaria, "How to Restore the American Dream," *Time*, Oct. 21, 2010.

85 *Fast Company* article: Anya Kamenetz, "Why Education without Creativity Isn't Enough," *Fast Company*, Sept. 14, 2011.

85 Vinod Khosla: Vinod Khosla (co-founder, Sun Microsystems), in discussion with the author, Sept. 9, 2014.

86 2012 industry report: Michael Masnick and Michael Ho, *The Sky Is Rising: A Detailed Look at the State of the Entertainment Industry* (Floor64, Redwood City, CA,

Jan. 2012), available at https://www.techdirt.com/skyisrising/.

87 experience of Dr. Irwin Braverman: See Christine DiGrazia, "Yale's Life-or-Death Course in Art Criticism," *New York Times*, May 19, 2002; and Holly Finn, "How to End the Age of Inattention," *Wall Street Journal*, June 1, 2012.

88 In 2013, the American Association of Colleges and Universities: *It Takes More Than a Major: Employer Priorities for College Learning and Student Success* (Washington, DC: Association of American Colleges and Universities and Hart Research Associates, 2013). The definition of *liberal education* read to survey participants was as follows: "This approach to a college education provides both broad knowledge in a variety of areas of study and knowledge in a specific major or field of interest. It also helps students develop a sense of social responsibility, as well as intellectual and practical skills that span all areas of study, such as communication, analytical, and problem-solving skills, and a demonstrated ability to apply knowledge and skills in real-world settings."

88 one recent study: Joan Burrelli, Alan Rapoport, and Rolf Lehming, "Baccalaureate Origins of S&E Doctorate Recipients" (InfoBrief, NSF 08–311, National Science Foundation, Division of Resources Statistics, Arlington, VA, July 2008), available at http://www.nsf.gov/statistics/infbrief/nsf08311/. Also see Thomas R. Cech, "Science at Liberal Arts Colleges: A Better Education?" *Daedalus* 128, no. 1 (Winter 1999): 195–216.

89 "So what does business need": Augustine, "One Cannot Live by Equations Alone."

90 "Get a liberal arts degree": Edgar M. Bronfman, "Business and the Liberal Arts," *Inside Higher Ed*, Oct. 17, 2013.

91 first-ever survey of the skills: Organisation for Economic Co-operation and Development, *OECD Skills Outlook 2013: First Results from the Survey of Adult Skills* (OECD Publishing, 2013).

91 most recent edition of the test: Organisation for Economic Co-operation and Development, *PISA 2012 Results: What Students Known and Can Do—Student Performance in Mathematics, Reading and Science* (Volume I, Revised edition, February 2014) (OECD Publishing, 2014).

91 United States has never performed especially well: See Elliott A. Medrich and Jeanne E. Griffith, *International Mathematics and Science Assessment: What Have We Learned?* (Washington, DC: U.S. Department of Education, National Center for Education Statistics, Feb. 1992), available at http://nces.ed.gov/pubs92/92011.pdf.

92 On average: Diane Ravitch, *Reign of Error: The Hoax of the Privatization Movement and the Danger to America's Public Schools* (New York: Knopf, 2013), 65. Ravitch makes the same point about historically poor American performance on international assessments, but she uses it as evidence that the U.S. education system does not require the kind of reforms now proposed by many, including the George W. Bush and Obama administrations. I would tend to disagree with that conclusion.

92 most recent assessment in the series: U.S. Department of Education, National Center for Education Statistics, Trends in International Mathematics and Sci-

ence (TIMSS), available at http://nces.ed.gov/timss/ (accessed Aug. 13, 2014).

92 United States spends more per capita: Organisation for Economic Co-operation and Development, *Education at a Glance 2014: OECD Indicators* (OECD Publishing, 2014), 204.

93 "We both have meritocracies": Tharman Shanmugaratnam quoted in Fareed Zakaria, "We All Have a Lot to Learn," *Newsweek*, Jan. 8, 2006. This quote also appeared in my book *The Post-American World* (New York: W. W. Norton, 2008).

93 It's not just Singapore: For more on the growing interest in the liberal arts in Asia, including the examples in this paragraph, see Yale-NUS College, *Yale-NUS College*, 14–22.

95 Israel actually ranks first: Organisation for Economic Co-operation and Development, *Entrepreneurship at a Glance* (OECD Publishing, 2014), 91. Also see the extremely interesting book by Dan Senor and Saul Singer, *Start-up Nation: The Story of Israel's Economic Miracle* (New York: Twelve, 2009).

95 2014 Bloomberg measure of technology density: "Most Innovative in the World 2014: Economies," *Bloomberg*, at http://www.bloomberg.com/visual-data/best-and-worst/most-innovative-in-the-world-2014-economies (accessed July 28, 2014).

95 Sweden and Israel performed: Organisation for Economic Co-operation and Development, *PISA 2012 Results*.

96 PISA tests don't simply evaluate students' skills: Organisation for Economic Co-operation and Development, *PISA 2012 Results: Ready to Learn: Students' Engage-*

ment, Drive and Self-Beliefs (Volume III) (OECD Publishing, 2013). PISA measured mathematics self-concept by asking students whether they agreed or disagreed with five statements, including "I learn mathematics quickly" and "I am just not good at mathematics." Table III.4.2a (p. 304) provides a country-by-country breakdown of the percentage of students indicating self-concept for each of the five questions. The overall ranking here was calculated by averaging the five separate rankings of countries by percentage.

96 "This country": William Bennett, *The De-Valuing of America: The Fight for Our Culture and Our Children* (New York: Summit Books, 1992), 42–43.

97 their book *The Triple Package*: Amy Chua and Jed Rubenfeld, *The Triple Package: How Three Unlikely Traits Explain the Rise and Fall of Cultural Groups in America* (New York: Penguin, 2014).

97 Some experts see no correlation: See, e.g., Keith Baker, "Are International Tests Worth Anything?" *Phi Delta Kappan* 89, no. 2 (Oct. 2007): 101–104.

97 while others point to data: See, e.g., Eric A. Hanushek and Ludger Woessmann, *The High Cost of Low Educational Performance: The Long-Run Impact of Improving PISA Outcomes* (OECD Publishing, 2010).

98 Scholars: Heiner Rindermann and James Thompson, "Cognitive Capitalism: The Effect of Cognitive Ability on Wealth, as Mediated through Scientific Achievement and Economic Freedom," *Psychological Science* 22, no. 6 (June 2011): 754–763.

98 America's top 1 percent intellectually: Jonathan Wai, "Of Brainiacs and Billionaires," *Psychology Today*, July 3, 2012.

99   "Over a long period of time": Thomas Piketty, *Capital in the Twenty-First Century* (Cambridge, MA: Belknap Press, 2014), 22.

100 On average, students in Shanghai: Bill Chappell, "U.S. Students Slide in Global Ranking on Math, Reading, Science," National Public Radio, Dec. 3, 2013, available at http://www.npr.org/blogs/thetwoway/2013/12/03/248329823/u-s-high-school-students-slide-in-math-reading-science.

100 U.S. Secretary of Education Arne Duncan: House Education and Labor Committee, *The Obama Administration's Education Agenda: Hearing before the Committee on Education and Labor*, 111th Cong. (May 20, 2009) (statement of Arne Duncan, Secretary of Education of the United States), 24, also available at http://votesmart .org/public-statement/427845/hearing-of-house-edu cation-and-labor-committee-the-obama-administra tions-education-agenda#.VCQ5UWRdVy8.

100 If Malcolm Gladwell is right: Malcolm Gladwell, *Outliers: The Story of Success* (New York: Little, Brown, 2008).

101 Jack Ma: C. Custer, "Jack Ma Explains Why China's Education System Fails to Produce Innovators," *Tech in Asia*, Dec. 9, 2014, available at https://www.techi nasia.com/jack-ma-explains-chinas-education-sys tem-fails-produce-innovators/.

101 academic year is much shorter: This has been the case for decades. *A Nation at Risk: The Imperative for Educational Reform* (Washington, DC: National Commission on Excellence in Education, 1983)—an influential report on the state of American education released under President Ronald Reagan—recommended that

school districts and state legislatures "strongly consider" increasing the length of the school year to between 200 and 220 days, in line with many other industrialized nations. There is some dispute, however, over how the American school year compares with school years in other countries. See, e.g., Jim Hull and Mandy Newport, "Time in School: How Does the U.S. Compare?" Center for Public Education, Dec. 2011, available at http://www.centerforpubliceducation.org/Main-Menu/ Organizing-a-school/Time-in-school-How-does-the-US-compare.

102 2010 research paper: Philip S. Babcock and Mindy Marks, "The Falling Time Cost of College: Evidence from Half a Century of Time Use Data" (National Bureau of Economic Research Working Paper No. 15954, Apr. 2010), available at http://www.nber.org/papers/w15954.

102 important new study: Richard Arum and Josipa Roksa, *Academically Adrift: Limited Learning on College Campuses* (Chicago: University of Chicago Press, 2010).

102 "Large numbers of four-year college students": "Frequently Asked Questions about *Academically Adrift*," Learning in Higher Ed, Social Science Research Council, at http://highered.ssrc.org/publications/academically-adrift/frequently-asked-questions/ (accessed Sept. 1, 2014).

103 Malcolm Gladwell: Malcolm Gladwell, interview by Fareed Zakaria, *Fareed Zakaria GPS*, CNN, July 21, 2013.

105 In late 1980s, at the peak of the belief: James Fallows, *More Like Us: Making America Great Again* (Boston: Houghton Mifflin, 1989).

4: The Natural Aristocracy

107 "our founding Yuppie": David Brooks, "Our Founding Yuppie," *Weekly Standard*, Oct. 23, 2000.

107 "would have felt right at home": Walter Isaacson,
   Benjamin Franklin: An American Life (New York:
   Simon & Schuster, 2003), 3.

107 In 1749, he published a pamphlet: Benjamin Franklin,
   Proposals Relating to the Education of Youth in Pennsylvania
   (Philadelphia, 1749), in *The Papers of Benjamin Franklin*,
   American Philosophical Society and Yale University, at
   http://franklinpapers.org/franklin// (accessed Sept. 17,
   2014). For more on Franklin's ideas about education,
   see Lorraine Smith Pangle and Thomas L. Pangle, *The
   Learning of Liberty: The Educational Ideas of the American
   Founders* (Lawrence: University Press of Kansas, 1993),
   75–90.

109 Franklin struggled: Isaacson, *Benjamin Franklin*, 147.
   For a more detailed look at this struggle, see a chapter
   in the late historian J. A. Leo Lemay's comprehensive
   yet unfinished biography *The Life of Benjamin Franklin*, vol. 3: *Soldier, Scientist, and Politician, 1748–1757*
   (Philadelphia: University of Pennsylvania Press,
   2008), 176–216.

109 Junto: Isaacson, *Benjamin Franklin*, 55–60.

110 "His work on electricity": Dudley Herschbach quoted
   in ibid., 129.

110 In 1778, Jefferson presented: Committee of the Virginia Assembly, "A Bill for the More General Diffusion of Knowledge," June 18, 1779, in *Jefferson Papers*,
   Founders Online, National Archives, http://found
   ers.archives.gov/about/Jefferson. For more on Jef-

ferson's ideas about education, see Pangle and Pangle, *Learning of Liberty*, 106–124.

111 "This would create": Michael Roth, *Beyond the University: Why Liberal Education Matters* (New Haven, CT: Yale University Press, 2014), 21–22.

111 "so thoroughly the work": Jon Meacham, *Thomas Jefferson: The Art of Power* (New York: Random House, 2012), 468.

112 University of Virginia was unique: "Jefferson's Vision of the Academical Village," University of Virginia, available at http://www.virginia.edu/academicalvillage/vision.html (accessed Sept. 24, 2014).

112 "natural aristocracy": Thomas Jefferson quoted in Roth, *Beyond the University*, 25–26.

112 "The best geniuses": Thomas Jefferson quoted in ibid.

113 "The whole people must take": John Adams quoted in ibid., 25. For more on Adams's view about education, see Pangle and Pangle, *Learning of Liberty*, 91–105.

114 What would they make of a country: Thomas B. Edsall, "The Reproduction of Privilege," *New York Times*, Mar. 12, 2012.

114 "The education system": Anthony Carnevale quoted in ibid.

115 As late as the 1970s, Berkeley's annual tuition: Larry Abramson, "Why Is College So Expensive?" *All Things Considered*, National Public Radio, Oct. 19, 2011, available at http://www.npr.org/2011/10/19/141505658/why-is-college-so-expensive.

115 For the 2014–15 academic year: Berkeley's cost of attendance can be found online at http://admissions.berkeley.edu/costofattendance.

116 "party pathway": Elizabeth A. Armstrong and Laura

T. Hamilton, *Paying for the Party: How College Maintains Inequality* (Cambridge, MA: Harvard University Press, 2013).

117 "I have to turn down": Admissions officer quoted in Fareed Zakaria, "The Thin-Envelope Crisis," *Time*, Apr. 15, 2013.

117 William Bowen: William Bowen and Sarah Levin, *Reclaiming the Game: College Sports and Educational Values* (Princeton, NJ: Princeton University Press, 2003). The original book on the same subject is James L. Shulman and William Bowen, *The Game of Life: College Sports and Educational Values* (Princeton, NJ: Princeton University Press, 2001). *Reclaiming the Game* has more current statistics that overwhelmingly prove Bowen's thesis.

117 2012 essay in the *American Conservative*: Ron Unz, "The Myth of American Meritocracy," *American Conservative*, Dec. 2012.

118 in comparison: Ibid.

118 *The Chosen*: Jerome Karabel, *The Chosen: The Hidden History of Admission and Exclusion at Harvard, Yale, and Princeton* (Boston: Houghton Mifflin, 2005).

119 average college tuition: Michelle Jamrisko and Ilan Kolet, "College Tuition Costs Soar: Chart of the Day," *Bloomberg*, Aug. 18, 2014.

120 Why has the cost of college risen so quickly?: William Baumol and William Bowen first introduced their cost disease theory in *Performing Arts, The Economic Dilemma: A Study of Problems Common to Theater, Opera, Music, and Dance* (New York: Twentieth Century Fund, 1966).

121 "while productivity gains": Robert H. Frank, "The

Prestige Chase Is Raising College Costs," *New York Times*, Mar. 10, 2012, quoted in William Bowen, *Higher Education in the Digital Age* (Princeton, NJ: Princeton University Press, 2013), 4.

121 Bowen points out: For Bowen's strong account of costs and productivity in higher education, first delivered as a Tanner Lecture on Human Values at Stanford University in 2012, see *Higher Education in the Digital Age*, 1–27.

123 *Academically Adrift*: Richard Arum and Josipa Roksa, *Academically Adrift: Limited Learning on College Campuses* (Chicago: University of Chicago Press, 2010).

124 By early 2014, the two main platforms: Fiona M. Hollands and Devayani Tirthali, "MOOCs: Expectations and Reality" (Center for Benefit-Cost Studies of Education, Teachers College, Columbia University, May 2014), 57.

126 2013 survey: Doug Lederman and Scott Jaschik, "Survey of Faculty Attitudes on Technology," *Inside Higher Ed*, Aug. 27, 2013.

127 Two recent studies: University of Pennsylvania Graduate School of Education, "Penn GSE Study Shows MOOCs Have Relatively Few Active Users, with Only a Few Persisting to Course End," Dec. 5, 2013, available at http://www.gse.upenn.edu/pressroom/pressreleases/2013/12/penn-gse-study-shows-moocs-have-relatively-few-active-users-only-few-persisti; and Andrew Dean Ho, Justin Reich, Sergiy O. Nesterko, Daniel Thomas Seaton, Tommy Mullaney, Jim Waldo, and Isaac Chuang, "HarvardX and MITx: The First Year of Open Online Courses, Fall 2012–Summer 2013" (HarvardX and MITx Working Paper No. 1, Jan. 21,

2014), 2, available at http://papers.ssrn.com/s013/papers.cfm?abstract_id=2381263.

127 media used these low completion rates: See, e.g., Tamar Lewin, "After Setbacks, Online Courses Are Rethought," *New York Times*, Dec. 10, 2013.

127 Coursera reports: Richard Levin (CEO, Coursera), in discussion with the author, Aug. 30, 2014.

128 In 2012 and 2013, approximately 43,000 students: Ho et al., "HarvardX and MITx," 2.

128 Robert Shiller: Levin, discussion with author.

129 Minerva Project: For more on the Minerva Project, see Graeme Wood, "The Future of College?" *Atlantic*, Aug. 13, 2014.

130 *The One World Schoolhouse:* Salman Khan, *The One World Schoolhouse: Education Reimagined* (New York: Twelve, 2012).

132 Stamenka Uvalić-Trumbić: Stamenka Uvalić-Trumbić, Remarks at the Closing Session of the UNESCO Global Forum on Rankings and Accountability in Higher Education (Paris, France, May 17, 2011), available at http://www.col.org/resources/speeches/2011presentation/Pages/2011–05–16.aspx.

132 "Inevitably, the greatest impact of MOOCs": Levin, discussion with author.

132 Already, 72 percent: Ho et al., "HarvardX and MITx," 25.

133 The vast majority: Ibid.; and Gayle Christensen, Andrew Steinmetz, Brandon Alcorn, Amy Bennett, Deirdre Woods, and Ezekiel J. Emanuel, "The MOOC Phenomenon: Who Takes Massive Open Online Courses and Why?" (working paper, University of Pennsylvania, Nov. 6, 2013), available at

http://papers.ssrn.com/s013/papers.cfm?abstract_id=2350964.

133 study published in November 2013: Christensen et al., "MOOC Phenomenon," 11. The 34,779 survey respondents were allowed to choose all reasons for enrolling that applied among four options. The results were as follows: "Curiosity, just for fun" (50.05 percent), "Gain specific skills to do my job better" (43.9 percent), "Gain specific skills to get a new job" (17.0 percent), and "Gain knowledge to get my degree" (13.2 percent).

5: Knowledge and Power

135 Prometheus brought fire: Ingri D'Aulaire and Edgar D'Aulaire, *D'Aulaires' Book of Greek Myths* (New York: Delacorte Press, 1992).

136 Aeschylus's version: Aeschylus, *Prometheus Bound*, ed. Alan Weissman, trans. George Thomson (New York: Dover Thrift, 1995).

136 So did Adam and Eve: Genesis 2–3, King James Version.

137 "ignorance is bliss": Thomas Gray, "Ode on a Distant Prospect of Eton College" (1747), in *Thomas Gray Archive*, available at http://www.thomasgray.org/cgi-bin/display.cgi?text=odec#panel_poem (accessed Sept. 15, 2014).

138 "drawn to the pursuit of knowledge": Cicero quoted in John Henry Newman, "Knowledge Its Own End," in *The Idea of a University* (London: Longmans, Green, 1907), 104, available at http://newmanreader.org/works/idea/discourse5.html.

138 "Other species": Richard Dawkins, "Apes with Big Brains: Richard Dawkins on What Makes Us Human," *New Statesman*, Jan. 6, 2014.

139 "a singular creature": Jacob Bronowski, *The Ascent of Man* (London: BBC Books, 2011), 19.

140 "Science": Bertrand Russell wrote often about science and philosophy, most extensively in *Religion and Science* (Oxford, UK: Oxford University Press, 1997). The quotes here come from a 1959 interview he did with the British journalist Woodrow Wyatt, available at https://archive.org/details/BertrandRussellDiscussesPhilosophy. The interview was part of a series with Wyatt, later published in book form as *Bertrand Russell Speaks His Mind* (1960).

141 Aristotle's explanation: See Aristotle, *Generation of Animals*, trans. A. L. Peck (Loeb Classical Library No. 366) (Cambridge, MA: Harvard University Press, 1942), 4.1.766a.

141 Charles II: Charles Panati, *Panati's Extraordinary Endings of Practically Everything and Everybody* (New York: Harper & Row, 1989), 265–267; and "Source Analysis—Death of Charles II Based on Scarburgh's Description," GSCE Bitesize, BBC News, available at http://www.bbc.co.uk/schools/gcsebitesize/history/shp/middleages/earlymodernsurgeryrev5.shtml (accessed Sept. 15, 2014).

142 Life expectancy: For historical life expectancy, see S. Ryan Johansson, "Medics, Monarchs and Mortality, 1600–1800: Origins of the Knowledge-Driven Health Transition in Europe" (Discussion Papers in Economic and Social History, No. 85, University of Oxford, Oct. 2010). For current life expectancy, see World Development Indicators, The World Bank, available at http://

data.worldbank.org/data-catalog/world-development-indicators.

142 United Nations estimated: United Nations Development Programme, *Human Development Report 1997* (Oxford, UK: Oxford University Press, 1997), 2.

142 average Chinese person today: World Development Indicators, The World Bank. Chinese life expectancy at birth rose from 45 years in 1962 to 75 in 2012. Chinese GDP per capita (in 2005 U.S. dollars) increased from $88.24 in 1963 to $3,583.38 in 2013. The multiple of 40 depends on whether you use inflation-adjusted or current dollars, as well as market-exchange or purchasing-power parity.

143 In 1960, nearly one in five children: World Development Indicators, The World Bank. The under-five mortality rate per 1,000 live births globally declined from 182.7 in 1960 to 45.6 in 2013.

143 It is quite possible: See, e.g., Jeffrey D. Sachs, "The End of Poverty, Soon," *New York Times*, Sept. 24, 2013.

143 Matt Ridley: Matt Ridley, *The Rational Optimist: How Prosperity Evolves* (New York: HarperCollins, 2011).

144 "humanitarian revolution": Steven Pinker, *The Better Angels of Our Nature: Why Violence Has Declined* (New York: Viking Books, 2011), 129–188.

144 "rights revolutions": Ibid., 378–481.

144 Some humanists balk: See, e.g., Donald Kagan, "Ave atque Yale," *New Criterion*, June 2013.

146 "the subjects of our study think": Herbert Simon quoted in Fareed Zakaria, "Blood Lust in Academia," *New Republic*, July 27, 1987, 16–18.

148 Nicholas Kristof has pointed: Nicholas Kristof, "Don't Dismiss the Humanities," *New York Times*, Aug. 13, 2014.

6: In Defense of Today's Youth

150 make a life: The phrase "Making a Living, Making a Life" comes from a wonderful commencement address delivered by Daniel Rose in 1986 at the Massachusetts Institute of Technology's Center for Real Estate Development. It is now included in a book of essays by Rose: *Making a Living, Making a Life* (Essex, NY: Half Moon Press, 2014).

151 "The Me Me Me Generation": Joel Stein, "Millennials: The Me Me Me Generation," *Time*, May 20, 2013.

151 "Crew practice at dawn": David Brooks, "The Organization Kid," *Atlantic*, April 2001.

152 "At the top of the meritocratic ladder": Ibid.

152 In 2014, the essayist: William Deresiewicz, *Excellent Sheep: The Miseducation of the American Elite and the Way to a Meaningful Life* (New York: Free Press, 2014).

153 "entitled little shit[s]": Ibid., 221.

153 notion that young people: See Meyer Reinhold, "The Generation Gap in Antiquity," and Barry Baldwin, "Young and Old in Imperial Rome," in Stephen Berman, ed., *The Conflict of Generations in Ancient Greece and Rome* (Amsterdam: John Benjamins, 1976), 15–54, 221–234.

154 Christopher Lasch: Christopher Lasch, *The Culture of Narcissism: American Life in an Age of Diminishing Expectations* (New York: W. W. Norton, 1979).

154 his 1987 book: Allan Bloom, *The Closing of the American Mind: How Higher Education Has Failed Democracy and Impoverished the Souls of Today's Students* (New York: Simon & Schuster, 1987).

154 Anthony Kronman: See Anthony Kronman, *Education's End: Why Our Universities and Colleges Have Given Up on the Meaning of Life* (New Haven, CT: Yale University Press, 2007).

157 Professor Steven Pinker: See Steven Pinker's response to Deresiewicz, in "The Trouble with Harvard: The Ivy League Is Broken and Only Standardized Tests Can Fix It," *New Republic*, Sept. 4, 2014.

157 UCLA's Higher Education Research Institute: See *The American Freshman: National Norms*, a series of annual reports presenting data on college freshmen, published by the Higher Education Research Institute at the University of California, Los Angeles. Reports dating to the 1960s are available at http://www.heri.ucla.edu/tfsPublications.php.

157 Over the last four decades: J. H. Pryor, S. Hurtado, V. B. Saenz, J. L. Santos, and W. S. Korn, *The American Freshman: Forty Year Trends, 1966–2006* (Los Angeles: Higher Education Research Institute, UCLA, April 2007), 31–34.

158 numbers who volunteer: See the Peace Corps press release "The Peace Corps Announces Record-Breaking Application Numbers in 2014," Oct. 8, 2014; and the Corporation for National and Community Service press release "AmeriCorps Week Marked from Coast to Coast," Mar. 23, 2012.

158 Teach for America: See the Teach for America press release "Teach for America Announces Record Number of Teachers for 2008," May 14, 2008. In a press kit, Teach for America reports that the organization received over fifty thousand applications for the 2014 teaching corps.

158 cover story in *Time* magazine: Stein, "Millennials."

159 "The incidence of narcissistic personality disorder": Ibid.

159 Elspeth Reeve: Elspeth Reeve, "Every Every Every Generation Has Been the Me Me Me Generation," *Wire*, May 9, 2013, available at http://www.thewire.com/national/2013/05/me-generation-time/65054/.

159 quote from the 2010 study: Brent W. Roberts, Grant Edmonds, and Emily Grijalva, "It Is Developmental Me, Not Generation Me," *Perspectives on Psychological Science* 5, no. 1 (Jan. 2010): 97–102.

159 2014 Nielsen report: *Millennials: Breaking the Myths* (New York: Nielsen, 2014). Some of the data in the Nielsen report come from the 2012 edition of the Achieve and Case Foundation study cited below.

160 study of the group sponsored by the Case Foundation: *Inspiring the Next Generation Workforce: The 2014 Millennial Impact Report* (Achieve and the Case Foundation, 2014), available at http://cdn.trustedpartner.com/docs/library/AchieveMCON2013/MIR_2014.pdf.

160 In a "TED Talk": Scott Hess, "Millennials: Who They Are and Why We Hate Them" (TEDxSF, June 2011), available at https://www.youtube.com/watch?v=P-en HH-r_FM.

160 In a talk at Princeton: David Brooks, "Politics and the Organization Kid" (Stafford Little Lectures at Princeton University, Princeton, NJ, Nov. 26, 2012), available at https://mediacentral.princeton.edu/media/1_b7 in7m0e.

161 billionaire-founder of LinkedIn: Reid Hoffman, *The Start-up of You: Adapt to the Future, Invest in Yourself, and Transform Your Career* (New York: Crown Business, 2012).

161 Some things the young don't do: See Abby Kiesa, Alexander P. Orlowski, Peter Levine, Deborah Both, Emily Hoban Kirby, Mark Hugo Lopez, and Karlo Barrios Marcelo, *Millennials Talk Politics: A Study of College Student Political Engagement* (Medford, MA: Center for Information and Research on Civic Learning and Engagement, Nov. 2007).

162 most striking result from the HERI survey: Pryor et al., *American Freshman: Forty Year Trends*, 33; and K. Eagan, J. B. Lozano, S. Hurtado, and M. H. Case, *The American Freshman: National Norms Fall 2013* (Los Angeles: Higher Education Research Institute, UCLA, 2013), 40.

163 In 1983, ABC aired a television movie: *The Day After*, directed by Nicholas Meyer (New York: ABC, 1983).

166 His speeches and blog posts: See posts by Bill Gates on http://www.gatesnotes.com.

167 "morally inarticulate": See, e.g., Brooks, "Politics and the Organization Kid." Also see David Brooks, "If It Feels Right . . . ," *New York Times*, Sept. 12, 2011.

168 HERI survey data: For the most recent figures, see Eagan et al., *American Freshman*, 40.

169 "I must study politics and war": Letter from John Adams to Abigail Adams, May 12, 1780, in *Adams Family Papers: An Electronic Archive*, Massachusetts Historical Society, available at http://www.masshist.org/digital adams/.

Acknowledgments

My first debt is to the president and trustees of Sarah Lawrence College, who asked me to deliver the commencement address to the Class of 2014. Thinking about the special qualities of that wonderful school, nestled in the suburbs of Manhattan, I decided to present a brief defense of a liberal education. I was surprised by the response, which went far beyond Sarah Lawrence, even beyond graduates of liberal arts programs. I realized that many people were thinking about these same issues and perhaps it would be useful to develop my ideas more fully and in print. So, I decided to write this book.

That's where Drake McFeely, my editor at W. W. Norton, came in. He was instantly enthusiastic about the idea and decided to move production along at a brisk pace, maintaining his gentlemanly manner even while he was cracking the whip (ably assisted in both regards by Jeff Shreve). This is my third book with Drake, and working with him has been one of the great professional pleasures of my life. Tina Bennett, my wonderful agent, handled every aspect of the book with her usual mixture of talent, dedication, and charm.

Gavan Gideon, fresh out of Yale College, helped me with the research on this book. Gavan leaped into this project after I had begun writing, and he was able to get up to speed so fast it startled me. In addition to being an excellent researcher, Gavan is a lucid writer and skilled editor and helped me shape the final manuscript. John Cookson, who used to work with me at CNN, has been an invaluable help as well, always expert at finding new sources of data and often discovering an interesting book or essay that I might have missed. John is a graduate of the University of Pennsylvania and Columbia University. If these are the products of a liberal education nowadays, we have nothing to worry about.

Working on a project like this while having a day job means relying on others for much help. Jessica del Pilar organized my life with an efficiency and intelligence that I could never match and a grace that I don't possess. After many years of helping me, she's moved on to bigger and better things at Washington University in St. Louis. Melanie Galvin has settled in as my assistant and is already making herself invaluable. Television takes more work than most people realize, and as the person in front of the camera, I get too much credit. The ones who deserve much more are the team at CNN that produces my show, *Fareed Zakaria GPS*: Tom Goldstone, Ravi Agrawal, Sujata Thomas, Maite Amorebieta, Dan Logan, Jessica Gutteridge, Nicole Boucher, and Dana Sherne. (Ravi and Sujata have also moved ahead in their careers.) In addition, a big thank you to Jeff Zucker for all his guidance and help. Fred Hiatt, who runs the *Washington Post*'s superb editorial pages, has always been a source of encouragement and support, even though he is often exasperated by my views on foreign policy. David Bradley at the *Atlantic* has been a friend, philosopher, and guide.

Providing life support is my wife, Paula, who has always encouraged me to work on the things that I love. She manages to keep our family running and thriving and is now turning to her own ambitions and considerable talents as a writer (and a graduate of Sarah Lawrence's MFA program, which is why I was invited to speak at the college). I owe her more than I can express.

Emerson once wrote, "It is one of the blessings of old friends that you can afford to be stupid with them."

I have afforded myself that pleasure many times. I turned fifty recently and, looking back, realized that what has given me the greatest joy in life has been my family and friends who have surrounded me with companionship and affection. The youngest members in that group are my three children, to whom this book is dedicated. My wife says that before you have children, you imagine that you want them to grow up and become presidents and prime ministers. Once they are in front of you, all you wish for is that they be happy and fulfilled—and live close by! That's my hope and prayer.